Autistically Speaking

Written By **Chelby Morgan**

ISBN: 978-16191-0030-5
LCCN: Library of Congress Control Number: 2020922453

The book identified above is exclusively published by Fycore Publishing in CA. It may be available for purchase at Walmart, Barnes & Noble, Amazon, Apple Books, and any other authorized Book Sellers. Contact Fycore Publishing to see if this title is available in other formats below.

CLOTH | HARD BACK | SOFT BACK | PDF | EPUB | COMIC BOOK | AUDIO BOOK

For product information, or permission to use copyrighted assets from this book, submit all request to Fycore Publishing.

131 Sunset Ave Ste E#353
Suisun City CA, 94585
Office | (800) 470-FYCORE
Facsimile:| (800) 558-8170
Email: | publisher@fycore.com
web: | **www.fycore.com**

Very Special Thanks:

First and foremost, to my Mom Erika and my Pop Mike, all I can say is, you are the best and I could not ask for better parents. I love you both more than I can express.

I want to thank my sister Taylor and two brothers, Mateo and Quinton. You all have been the best siblings a person could ever ask for and I thank you and love you all.

I also want to thank all of my immediate family members who have been instrumental in my life. You all have been ones I look up to and I greatly appreciate all of your patience you've shown me and the support you provided. I also want to give this special thanks to my Nanny (grandmother) who is an inspiration to me.

I can't forget to thank my case worker Ms. Lilly, and my ParaPro's Tabbitha Crueger, Ms. Condrey, Michelle Garcia, Denise Liam, Ms. Blanche Washington. I appreciate you all being my One To One aides and the services you provided that helped me get through all of my school years. I also want to thank North Bay Regional Center for the supportive services they provided to me and my peers. To the rest of my dear close friends, I also thank you for being true friends.

I last want to thank my Publisher who believed in me and helped me to get my book out to the world. Thank you and thank you all.

Warmest Regards,
Chelby Morgan

Foreword

To my delight, I was asked by Fycore Publishing to interview Ms. Chelby Morgan. I found Ms. Morgan to be a remarkable woman having a personality of great interest.

During her interview Ms. Morgan related the challenges of writing her memoirs and getting published. Having reached out to many Publishers by mail, phone, and email, she expressed how difficult it was to locate a publisher and how no one seemed to have time for her especially during the current world pandemic. Quiet as kept, writing memoirs, and finding a publisher can be a difficult challenge for all Authors.

After many attempts, she received an email reply from Fycore Publishing, who invited her to a Zoom interview regarding her manuscripts. Her interview resulted in a great success where she was assured to become a published author. This coincidentally was a lifelong dream of hers.

Not fully understanding the milestone she had reached, she did something remarkable during finalizing her book deal. Modestly, her only desire was to see her book sold through her favorite bookstore, Barnes & Noble. The Publisher chuckled when indicating to Ms. Morgan, her book would be sold and distributed everywhere books are sold in over 40,000 different stores and over 190 Countries around the world including Barnes & Noble. Subsequently, her book was also inducted into The Library of Congress.

Who said persistence does not pay off! Ms. Morgan desires anyone impacted by a disability to know, they too can thrive. Her positive attitude convinced me that failure is defeated the moment a person makes effort to achieve any goal they set. This book is now one of my favorite books to read. It was my honor to interview Ms. Morgan, writer of **Autistically Speaking.** Ms. Morgan you now have our undivided attention.

Foreword by
Victoria E. Kain

TABLE OF CONTENTS

Author: Chelby Morgan

CHAPTER 1

My Childhood

My Childhood

I was born in Vallejo California to loving parents. When I was a baby I remember how everyone was always crazy about me and always wanted to do stuff for me and give me presents as well. I vividly remember allot of stuff about me when I was a baby. I even have proof of it in one of my favorite pictures that's in a frame of me being held by my mother. In the picture my mom was very happy to hold me and she had a nice smile on her face. I had on a floral dress with a matching hat.

There are tons of pictures of my sister when she was a baby. I noticed her lips are almost like the lips I had when I was little. As a baby there was a lot that I enjoyed getting done for me such as a hair wash which I also have a picture in my stash that my parents also have in their possession. This is a wonderful memory.

My mom was always smiling when she was washing my hair. That was always a happy time. Now I will jump to when I was three, the diagnosis for autism came in. From that point on services for me were made in my behalf. The autism that I was diagnosed with did not stop me from learning how to walk, talk, formulate sentences, and use the bathroom, but I will say it did take me a few extra years and a little while longer than usual to learn even what is considered basic things.

Author: Chelby Morgan

I will share with you that by the time I was five I was almost going to the bathroom by myself without any needed assistance. Go me! Also when I was five, Dr noticed I suffered from Echolalia, which im told is a form of behavior where I was repeating everything that everyone was saying. So if I repeat myself in my book and jump around in thought please don't trip don't trip. That last one was a joke :)

Guess what. I am my own editor so don't worry though, I used spell check in my book and the one that is on Microsoft word. I'm not sure if it catches everything so if it doesn't then I'm blaming them.

Anyway despite me being Autistic or artistic as I prefer to call it, that still did not stop me from growing or living normally as possible. With the help of my family, I did learn to phase out certain behaviors. I worked hard not to repeat things that was said made no sense to repeat. Again, from my POV, by the way POV means point of view.

Whatever I repeated seemed normal to me. I went to an elementary school. I forgot the name of it because it's been a long time since I've been in elementary school. I forgot the name of because it's been a long time.

Anyway, when I went to that school that I forgot the name of, I was in a class where you could do art, paint, and play with Play-Doh which was my favorite thing to do.

I loved Play-Doh because I was able to make shapes and sizes and pound it altogether. I liked Play-Doh so much I even tried to eat it but the teacher stopped me and told my mom on me. Then my mom said not to eat Play-Doh. At the time I did not fully understand why I could not eat Play-Doh but obviously it is not good to do and dangerous, so I did not do it anymore since then.

But one of the reasons I really stopped trying to eat Play Doh was because I will never forget how my uncle told me not to eat Play Doh or I would turn into Play Doh. Well I didn't love Play Doh that much and did not want to turn into it. When I got older he did eventually tell me that he was just kidding about turning into Play Doh , part he wanted me to not want to turn into it and not eat it. I have to say that it worked because I did not want to turn into Play Doh and I never ate it again. I did still play with it tho .

I also remember that being a kindergartner was really fun because I also got to play all day and be on the swings at the indoor playground that I remember that my class would do all the time. I didn't have any extra work, and it seemed all I did was just show up for class and get to play, do art, play on the swings, play with the Play-Doh (he he he) and just listen to my teacher teach my class.

Fast forward, some of my fellow classmates in kindergarten were the same kids that I had in my fourth and half of my fifth-grade class.

Author: Chelby Morgan

At the time I had no idea they also had the same disability that I have, but theirs was even more severe side because they could not talk, formulate sentences, retain information that they read in books. They also could not go to the bathroom by themselves. Like me they could not handle themselves in regular classroom settings.

I only realized all of that from being in class with them. It's funny because even though I suffered from the same disability, there disability seemed obvious to me they had issues while I did not realize I also had the same autism just not as severe and mine did not prevent me from being able to do certain things.

I have a picture of me in a nice sunflower dress with a big flower in the center of my jean dress and big smile on my face and to this day I still have that picture. Sometimes when my mom looks at the picture, she's says "That's my sugar." I liked that because I was her firstborn and I shine like the sun.

To this day I still consider it a privilege to be the firstborn child and grandchild because one thing I have learned is even with any disabilities, advantages will always override disadvantages.

When I was still five, that's when I remember my sister came into the picture and she was just the cutest baby ever. I looked at her arrival as an advantage.

I was never jealous of her or resentful because she was the best thing that I could ever have besides my Barbie dolls and dresses.

I loved my sister so much because she was the best sister anyone could ever have. If you see pictures of her when she was a baby you would love her too.

When she started to walk, she would always have the biggest grin on her face like the Kool aid mascot while she would hold her pacifier in her mouth with her beautiful face and eyes to top it off. She was beautiful then and she still is today. As a matter of fact, I have a picture of her when she was a baby as a screen saver so that I could always remember her that way.

Now when it came to food it was kinda a different story. I remember one time when I had some popcorn, I would hoard some for myself because I had to share it with her once she had teeth and was able to start eating big people food. She was such a cutie pie, so I did give her some of my popcorn. Another funny thing was I tried to try on her little itty-bitty sandals but my feet were too big for them, so I had to take them off. I wanted my feet to be small like hers.

Then when I was seven we moved to a nice house in Las Vegas and that was when my baby brother came into the picture and oh my goodness, he too was by far the second cutest baby boy in the whole wide world. I mean he had chubby cheeks, turkey legs, curly hair, and was oh so adorable in his onesies which to this day has proven to be one of my favorite clothing for a baby to wear.

As a matter of fact, I like when babies wear onesies. It accentuates the chubby figures that they have going on so if I see a baby with a onesie on, then I really like that because them wearing that clothing makes them look oh so cute.

My brother was also the best brother that I've ever had because I got to love and value him as the beloved little brother that I have always known him to be. I always wondered what he would be and look like when he got older because I had a curious mind for a child my age back then. My brother loved his father because when he got held by his father, he would just have the biggest grin on his face. I love my brother down to this day even though I at times miss the chubby little guy that he used to be though.

That same year in Las Vegas where we lived, I had a teacher that was very mean to me. At the time she didn't know I was autistic so whenever I did just about anything she did not understand, she would put me in the corner. One time I didn't want to get out of the corner and decided to stay there until she had to walk over there and get me out. That teacher got on my nerves and at that time I understood what that meant because she did get on my nerves. Keep in mind all of this was before I could speak clearly. I knew what I wanted to say as many autistic children do but, some times I could not get the words out to fully say it.

Although I knew I was different, I caught on to the fact that my mom was not going to let me get away with anything like I saw the other kids with disabilities at school getting away with.

You know the screaming and yelling and throwing things. When a disabled person see's people treating us different, we do sometimes take advantage of it. We call it playing the D card.

I even tried to play the D card at my uncle's house when he would not let me play with Play Doh. I called myself throwing a fit and screaming as loud as I could. I will never forget what my uncle said. He said *"chelby what's all this noise? I no you ain't acting crazy caz you bout to catch a beat down. I suggest you knock it off if you don't want a beat down..."* I remember telling my uncle that I don't want a beat down and he telling me I never have to worry about one from him as long as I acted like I had sense. It made sense to me, and I always acted right, at least around him.

For some reason, I never wanted to test him and knocked off my nonsense whenever he came around. I remember telling my uncle how I didn't like my teacher at school. He then asked me, what did me not liking my teacher have to do with butter. He then told me to go to the refrigerator for the answer. When I saw the butter I did not understand how the butter made any difference with me not liking my teacher. He said that was the point. Not liking my teacher has nothing to do with going to school and I had better learn to like my teacher if did not want to see her again for the next year.

Author: Chelby Morgan

That was all the motivation I needed. My uncle was what you would call a straight shooter. He would never let me slide on anything and would say, "if you think imma let you slide, it will be after I'm sliding to the left doing the James Brown." I figured out a way to get out of trouble if my uncle was around. I noticed that whenever I made him laugh, that's how I could get out of trouble.

It funny how when you are a kid everyone who raises their voice seems intimidating. In reality my uncle has always been the nicest person in the world to me.

My parents on the other hand thought my teacher was awesome and I didn't know why. Now that I think about it, my teacher must have understood that I realized more than I let on. Whenever I was doing anything I was not supposed to do, she'd call my parents on me and that usually corrected me.

When we moved to Las Vegas, it was fun to live there. Needless to say I was glad when we moved out of Las Vegas to Stockton California. That was a trip. By trip I mean it in the negative street vernacular sense. Such as if I were to say "you tripping."

When we moved from Vegas to Stockton my cover was blown! We took a train to transfer to the city where we were going. When we got to Stockton, we moved into a two-bedroom apartment that we had to get organized and settled into before we could do anything else.

Come to find out, I now had to share a room with my sister and my brother. By this time, I realized and already saw on TV that all kids should have there own rooms. I didn't like sharing a room and felt I deserved my own bedroom. For me to have to share a bedroom with was not going to go down very well.

In a short period of time I got used to it. By short period of time, I mean within 5 minutes I started to enjoy my sister's company. She on the other hand, had issues with me being in there with all of my abilities and repetitiveness that at times got on everyone's nerves as they expressed.

One thing I recall doing with my brother was we would look out of the window and watch dad get into his car and go to work. Dad was a hard worker and seemed to work all the time. Pop was the best and the nicest of all. When my sister said that he was going to work, my brother would pretend that he wasn't going to work and would contradict it and say Pop was home.

My sister would say yes he did go to work. Then they would argue about it. It went back and forth and was playful because it really wasn't all that serious to begin with. Sometimes we all would have the habit of looking out of the window just to watch Pop go to work and that became our game. Sometimes we would get bored of just sitting in our rooms because it may have been raining or it wasn't safe to be outside by ourselves and mom had work to do in the house.

Author: Chelby Morgan

One time when my brother was in his crib, I decided since I am the oldest, I would change his diaper and help out. That didn't turn out well because he smelled so stinky and I was not even halfway through. I realized I couldn't change him, because he was to stinky. I wondered how could someone so cute, stink so badly?

So I froze and would just stand there while he would laugh and sat waiting for a full diaper change. When my mom came in and saw the scene, she was not happy that I started to change him to begin with. I basically didn't know what I was doing. Fortunately, she fixed him and he was all clean again and didn't stink. My mom told me not to try and change his diaper anymore unless I could complete the job. That was one job I did not ever want to attempt again.

That lesson was learned. I was not going to be changing diapers until I really knew what I was doing and would be able to hold my breath for at least 2 min.

Around the time when I was nine, my family moved to Vallejo, California, my birthplace, and we settled into this wonderful home on that it had a garage, nice driveway, front door, three bedrooms, and a long sidewalk to ride our bikes on.

That was the time that I was learning to ride and balance on a bike without falling off. It took a while to learn to ride a bike but in time I mastered the technique with the help of my cousins.

That was also the time when my cousins who were around my same age as me came to my house for company. Once my they came over for a sleep over and that's when they showed me how to ride a bike since I was having a hard time. And boy, did she have that bike riding technique down. She rode that bike with no effort at all. Being nine was starting to be one of the best years of my childhood because I got closer to my cousins who were both living in Vallejo.

Once my cousins on my mom's side came to the office where my mom was working at the time, and we would go to a room that was designated for the children. It had TV and barbie dolls for us to play with. We even took turns sitting on the couch because sometimes one of us would hog the couch from each other. While my cousin was sitting on the couch, I'd be sitting on the floor just repeatedly messing up my cousin's name so much that she would tell me to stop making fun of her name.

I don't know how long I did that but it eventually stopped when I was a teenager. By that time I would just move on to messing up names just for the sake of repeating something. I guess it was part of my autistic behavior.

Also school was the best because I got to go to this one class where I could play around and do fun stuff with my class together so when I had that class in fifth grade and had to go to regular class, I was not happy because I enjoyed that class because I was being made to be responsible.

Author: Chelby Morgan

The tendency to play was still there but it was time to grow up. Fourth grade was fun because I got the best of both worlds where I was in the play classroom and the regular classroom at the same time. The regular classroom proved to be fun as well because I met some exciting individuals who helped me to be the social creature that I am right now.

They would make small talk with me and sometimes share their snacks with me. The conversation helped me to understand how to be sociable and I paid attention to the responses that they gave.

One time I ate some of a classmates' chips but the other student ratted me out so I had to owe her for snacks but it wasn't a big deal. I gave her the snacks that I owed her and the issue was resolved from that point on.

Sometimes, I would go to another classroom and I didn't want to go there because I was just getting used to being in that class, so for me to have to go from one regular class to another was not sitting well for me. When nobody was looking I decided to be late for that class on purpose and I never told my mom. Well if she is reading this then she knows now. Sorry mom.

Oh my goodness! One time when I had to go to the class by the street, I would intentionally be late for that class by walking across the playground that was right where the section for a kindergarten class.

The kindergarten section was the best because it had a playground and cute kindergarten children. Some kids who were part of the unwanted class that I had to go to were there and told me that I was late so they would go and tell the teacher.

By the time I got there, my teacher found out and told me that I was late. And if she did give me a consequence that I can't remember, it probably wouldn't have been much of a big deal because I'd probably do it again if I knew I'd get away from escaping a class that I didn't want to be in. Truth be told, it was really boring. For me to not go to that class proved to be a blessing especially when there was a special class that I could hang out and be taught everything the easy way. It seemed that I was trying to control how I was learning things. I simply wasn't ready to move on to the next phase.

After that day of intentionally being late for that class, I thought I was going to be able to do that again but I was wrong because two girls from that "unwanted class" came to escort me to her class. Let me explain the "unwanted" class. It was a class where I had to behave a certain way and I was not ready for that.

When they did, I tried to get away and hit one of the girls but they would win and get me to the class. To this day I don't remember what was really being taught but when I didn't have to go to that class in the fifth grade I was more than relieved because it was boring.

Author: Chelby Morgan

I have to be honest like that. When my teacher from the special class mentioned what was going on in this class and how it would help me, I would totally not look forward to it because it was really boring and no fun but the boring class did not happen at all. One student who heard me trying to whine my way out of going to the boring class would make a joke out of it and mess up her name saying:

I don't want to go to Miss Gelatti's class. He was one of the kids that I just did not like at all because he was very mean and always getting on my nerves, so I decided to mess with him from that point on. Once I missed out on a picnic that my other class was going to because I had to go to another class, so by the time I got back to the other class, I just missed out on the picnic and I was just not happy.

My fifth grade memories allowed me to go to the special class where I could play all day, read small books, and event eat in the classroom, have breakfast, gather around for goodbye songs, and go on special field trips together. I was having a good time in that class until my mom pulled me out of that class and had me in a regular class with a autistic Paraprofessional or ParaPro, who would guide me. When that happened, I was not very happy because I was just enjoying class for special kids. For me to be in a regular class proved to be a challenge at one point.

I had to do regular schoolwork and have homework on top of that as well and I would fight that at times because I wanted to be in a class where I could play around all day and not have to do any work. I mean I would fight my ParaPro on it because when I went to a regular class.

I had to do fractions, definitions and essays and one time when I didn't want to do any assignments and I actually refused, my parents would find and give me a warning about what would happen if I didn't do my assignments. Then I had to do fractions which I found to be very difficult because they were very complicated, and I even cried about it. I just didn't want to push myself to do it in the first place, so I just felt like giving up. I heard that my special class was moving to a portable room called T5. That being said, we were able to relocate to that class and see what it really looked like.

The classroom had a enough room to move about in and fit all their stuff in. Then it was time to go to the regular class so I was really looking for a way out of it especially when I had to do work that I just want to do at all. When it came to fractions, I would cry over it to the point where my aide had to pull me out of the class and tell me that we can go to T5 but I would still have to do the fractions so that was her way of telling me that I wasn't getting out of it.

Author: *Chelby Morgan*

So my way of getting out doing assignments that I didn't want to do wasn't going to work at all. All I herd in my head was "my uncle saying whats all this noise..." I basically had no choice but to do it and not cry over it. I missed that class very much because I didn't have to do hard work like fractions but at the same time I took for granted that I was able to communicate with my peers, teacher and even my aide for that matter. Even though I had an aide I was able to communicate my needs and wants with her and if I just wanted to talk, she was there to listen so I should've met her halfway a little bit better and done my part a little bit better as well.

As time went on, I started getting used to the class as the paragraphs that I had to write were starting to be a breeze because some of the subjects that were involved were quite easy so that was like an easy A for me.

Besides even though I couldn't play around all day long and do just the easy basic assignments, there were other things that I enjoyed such as social studies, field trips without baby trips to the fire station like was the case with some students from the special class that I used to be in along with fun stuff with my hair from a certain poem song about hair.

Speaking of hair, we wore funky hairstyles and performed in front of a live audience in the cafeteria.

Even when I wasn't in that class one time, I got to go to one hair shop to get my perm and flat iron done at a shop in Vallejo. I liked that part because my hair was getting longer, and I had been wanting to wear my hair down for the longest. Besides I think what it is that it prepared me for getting to the type of age where I had to do my own hair even though I didn't use a flat iron until I was either in my late teens or early 20s.

What was so funny about that is that I did my own hair in the sixth grade, but I never washed or conditioned my own hair; my mom still did that kind of hard hair labor. Then I started to appreciate being out of that special class because I was able to prepare for middle school and do basic braiding of my hair in middle school.

Then another thing that got me used to the class was silent reading which I enjoyed so much because one of the books that I liked to read was Pippi Long Stocking.

Pippi Long Stocking is that I enjoy reading down to this day because it just brings back wonderful childhood memories that I sometimes would love to go back to any day without the drama that comes with being a teenager.

One of the things that I like about Pippi Long Stocking that she was very carefree, easygoing and unconventional because she had her own agenda and wasn't fazed by any threats that people made towards her.

One time when authorities were trying to take her to a home for orphaned children, she put a fight because she wasn't having it.

Her strength was exceptional because she was the strongest girl that one town in Sweden knew her to be because if somebody tried to fight her they would not win because she would just drop them like a hot potato.

There was a story where Pippi was having a picnic with her friends Tommy and Annika and when a bull was coming their way because of the fact that he was not fond of children, Pippi would step in the way of the bull and put up a fight with the bull so bad that she rode the bull and would not let go even though he would try to get her off.

It was so funny because he thought he could just throw her off in no time but boy was he wrong because Pippi was strong enough to hold on so when she got done with him, he fell asleep and Pippi went home with her friends. That is one of my favorite books down to this day because I like books that remind me of a good childhood.

Fifth grade started to be fun as well because graduation came with me being to go to Denny's afterward. I was in a nice pink dress when I went. Then middle school would come. I will discuss that in my next chapter folks.

CHAPTER 2

Middle School Years

Middle School Years

Besides elementary school, middle school was also one of the best years of my life, because when I started middle school, the school had orientation to get us acquainted with the whole school. First I got to meet the school staff and one of the school staff that I met was a nice lady named Miss A because she was awesome.

When she worked as a counselor for the school, she was nothing but the best even when some of the students were sent to her office for punishment. I never was sent to her for any talking, even when the one time when I didn't want to do my assignments in class, my aide would suggest that we go there but it didn't happen because she ended up talking to me and settling the whole situation with me squarely.

I never even got referrals to a principal's office because I was now a good student for the majority of the time even though I had to step outside with my aide and get talked to about what went on with me in the classroom.

I do think that what got me saved from going to the principal's office was that I had an aide that would handle every matter with me by herself and would allow a punishment to fit a "crime" that I would "commit" so I never had any problems with being referred to a principal or counselor for that matter.

When orientation got started, every sixth grader got situated at the amphi-theater, a place where we would be eventually eating our lunches at but of course we would also have a choice to eat at the bench tables outside by food vendors or in the multi-purpose room where a small stage, tables and a lunch vendor would be at as well.

We were at the amphi-theater where a teacher would give a speech about what our new school would all about before going to the gym to enjoy music and a "motivational speech" from another teacher who was also a PE teacher for the school.

I at first didn't want to go outside but the nice counselor lady reassured me that it wouldn't be scary while she went with me to help me get myself settled and situated inside the gym.

After that, we sixth graders got to tour the whole school so that we would know where our classes, office, bathrooms and cafeteria are and would be on time for our class schedules that we were handed out to us as well.

We got our schedules for our classes and I don't know about anybody else but the classes that I had were the best because one, I had most women as teachers and two, the subjects that I had were one of my favorite subjects to have such as social studies and English.

Oh one time I had to go to the bathroom so went in there and while I was in there, another girl was running in the bathroom because I think that she was obviously playing.

Author: Chelby Morgan

I think it was with some other kid but the scene wasn't pretty because she ran around to the bathroom so bad that she hit her head on something. She then started crying because it started to hurt.

An adult saw her crying after she got hurt and told her that it was time for her to be responsible so there would be no more running around. I saw the whole scene and thought: "Well someone is probably not used to middle school adjustment". After we toured the whole school and the students and teachers said their goodbyes, the students went home and awaited their first day of school.

The first day of school came and I was just excited because I got to meet my first teacher and he was by farthest one of the best teachers that I've ever had. When I went into his class, we went over the rules together as a class and some of the rules that he went over were no foul language or hitting was allowed but you know how that went. Sooner or later the rules weren't followed and some of the teachers who knew about the rules that were broken.

They either tolerated it or just gave out inconsistent consequences for every rule that was broken. An example of that was when the teachers would hear some students using foul language, they would either listen to it or simply tell them to watch their language without any serious consequence to it so the students were basically allowed to say whatever they wanted.

The first class I had was called first period and it was a class where it involved warm-ups, science and curriculum support classes.

What I liked most about the class was science because we didn't have to do homework except science projects. To tell you the truth I did not like homework because I really wanted to go home, play, watch TV and play video games. I would have taken anything over homework any day.

Then I had social studies which I liked the best for I was able to study history from different countries such as China, a country that I always wanted to go to because it reminded of this character named Sawgwa from TV. She was a Siamese cat from China who had a brother and a sister along with her parents who lived in a beautiful house with the queen and majesty. Sawgwa had a brother named Dongwa and a sister that I just forgot the name but if I check out the program maybe the name will come up.

One of the things that they would do when they got up in the morning was write scrolls for the majesty and it was always these wonderful Chinese characters and calligraphy that the majesty would have them write which I now wonder about because it was like how could a cat write scrolls and they weren't even human at all.

Then at other times I would be thinking about how neat it would be for a cat to write Chinese scrolls on TV but a regular cat in real life can't do that. By now I already learned that what is real and what is not real so therefore I have to treat it as just that: just TV.

Another best part about the show was the cook and the majesty's assistant.

Author: Chelby Morgan

The cook was always serving the cats dumplings and noodles which I found to be very delicious because they look very authentic and scrumptious. I found myself wanting to try a dumpling and some noodles at it and that dream came true because later in life I got to try some dumplings and noodles from an authentic Chinese restaurant in New York.

Whenever Sawgwa came on I faithfully watched it because I found myself wanting to travel to China and try some Chinese food and just tour the whole country itself.

During social studies, the chapter that I was currently studying was about China which sparked my interest in traveling to China even more. I studied every inch of China that the whole chapter covered and I even had the best teacher because she was really nice. She always helped us study for our upcoming tests so that we could get good grades and be rewarded for it. I was really enjoying that class until she left and was replaced with another nice teacher who specialized in language arts.

One of the best things that she did was give us a pretest in spelling to test out our knowledge. She would have us number our papers from one to ten before giving us a word to write down. We would write down the word for each number that we numbered our papers and whatever word we misspelled we had to write it five times unless some of the students like me would correct them before the teacher even found out about it.

I did it to avoid having to write the right spelling word five times and yeah the teacher didn't know about it but another teacher did and it was called my aide who called me out on it and told that it was cheating and that I should've been honest about it. I didn't mean to be dishonest, but I also didn't want to write every misspelled letter five times.

But other times when there was a pretest for a spelling test and I got a spelling I had to correct it five times and in my own initiative I showed it to my mom and she encouraged me to keep trying my best to get every word right.

So, with that being said, when the teacher would schedule a day for our actual spelling test, she was giving us enough time to study all of our words before giving us the spelling. Man! That was so easy I aced all the spelling tests that came my way because I studied and tried my best at spelling all of the words correctly.

Spelling tests were the best because the words for them were really easy to study so I would always look forward to taking the test for them. Then when we had to study for other tests, the teacher would get the class together in groups to help us study and prepare for tests which I thought was helpful because when a group full of people help one another study and prepare for a test, then it really helps in going a long way in preparing and studying for an upcoming test that was to come up so that we could ace them all.

I studied them with the help of my parents even though I didn't always get some answers right the first time. At times when I got a test with a grade like a C or an F, I would always get to chance to correct the grade with a retesting and that worked out well because when I took a retest for every chapter and I corrected that grade, I would end up getting the best grade which would either get a B or an A.

One time, along with some other students who made good grades in the class got to have a little small party as a reward. We had cake and juice and stayed for a while during lunch time before going to our next class. The next class that I had was curriculum class and that was awesome because we got all the help that we need for homework, and classwork while we played games together as a class and did silent reading. As always, silent reading was always the best part of the class because I got to read whatever book that I wanted to read without the teacher specifying.

One time I got to borrow some of the books from another teacher's classroom but one time when I didn't want to do any reading, I decided to crinkle up the books in effort to rip them apart because I was really bored of reading. That didn't get any nice results because I had to write sentences while being escorted to the office to do my sentences and I would cry because I didn't want to write any of the sentences either.

Plus I was forbidden to borrow any of that teacher's books either even if she was my teacher. I got over that real quick because reading her books wasn't a big deal for me after all. The last parts that I mentioned was all my fault because I called myself not wanting to listen, so I basically reaped what I sowed.

Had I listened, that wouldn't have to happen, and I would've still been able to borrow her books. Anybody that said she was mean was wrong because they didn't give themselves a chance to really know her as a person and nowadays when people say things like that, it really irks me because I feel that people should not look at what's on the outside.

They should look on the insides before they start jumping to conclusions about other people. Last but not least, I had PE which really rocked, because I got to exercise and do some cool warm-ups like jumping jacks which I still loved to do down to this day because it really helps in lowering your muffin tops. I would do that any day that I had an opportunity to be outside or just do it for the sake of getting in an exercise when I am on my cycle.

My PE teacher was cool because we got play some basketball games with teams and I was always told to watch out for the opposite team because if I didn't they would fake me out in having me think that they were on my team but they wouldn't be if I lost to them. Also we didn't have to run like we did in seventh grade which I thought was nice because I did not like running until I turned 18.

Author: Chelby Morgan

Oh, case in point, I was in Junior High, but I was not like the other eleven year olds in my group because I wasn't thinking about boys, latest fashions or make-up. All I would be thinking about would to watch cartoons, play dolls with my sister and look at ants and pick up stuff off the ground.

Plus I had a wonderful baby brother with the biggest cheeks, fattest belly, and the biggest Kool-aid grin on his face. I mean he was always smiling at you and welcomed any entertainment that you had in mind for him because he was always smiling and had the best disposition that an older sibling could ever benefit from.

Sometimes I think that if he were a baby again, I would just be like a mother to him by hugging and cuddling him, keeping him company, entertaining his, feeding talking to him like a baby, and just taking care of him like an actual mother would take care of him with the only exception of changing his pamper.

I truly loved him and I knew he loved me too even though I felt that I could've done more for him at times like hold him, give him more company and just help out with him for that matter. Him coming into the world when I was 11, was the best thing that ever happened to me because now my love for babies has heightened.

Sixth grade came and gone which I was not happy because I missed the good times that sixth grade had to offer such as curriculum support for one classroom because when I got to seventh grade, I knew it would be the worst because I had issues to combat.

One of the things that always gave me issues was math and having to listen to the teacher talk about the subject because I was just bored and felt that the class was not something that I could really enjoy or gain anything out of.

I did take math notes but I hated doing problems and formulas such as functions because I felt like I wouldn't know how to do it so I would rely on my aide to help me solve most of the problems while letting me do the minimum of the work.

One time when I didn't want to really put some work into solving some of the problems of a function formula, I was told that I could get kicked out of the class and get a zero on both my class work and homework. If I did get kicked out of the classroom, I would either drop a tear and stand out there or just tell the teacher to just send me out of the class and let me take a zero before walking out of the classroom and off the campus all the way to the railroad tracks and beyond in order to avoid that class altogether.

I hated math to death and still do. I mean I wouldn't even do it to save my life. It turns out that I didn't get sent out of the classroom so I didn't have to worry about getting a zero on all of my schoolwork for math before storming out of the classroom and off campus to walk on the railroad tracks, meet up with young ones who have also decided to skip a class or school altogether, and just kick it before going to my next class.

Besides there was a time when kids didn't want to be in a certain class or just didn't like what the teacher was saying or teaching, they were able to leave the class because the teacher would give them that kind of option.

Even though I didn't do it, I welcomed and appreciated that option because for me it was a way out of class. I probably would've taken advantage of that option. Of course, if that happened, it wouldn't go well with me because I would've gotten in hot water with both my teacher and parents for, they would've expected something better out of me.

I think it was just me feeling my teenage hormones and they were raging. Plus I would've gotten a lecture from my parents and some restrictions added for my punishment. It turned out that I got a really good grade for that class and when my report card came, my parents were really proud. When that period ended, I was glad to get up out of that classroom and move to history which I loved with a passion.

I had a teacher who was very enthusiastic and passionate about history. She would get the class involved in special assignments such as doing writing assignments as groups together. She even had us march in a circle to music on a radio, learning different countries and borders on a map. We had weekly test to study. Although I did study for most of the test, I didn't get the best grade that I felt that I could've gotten.

Overall, I still got the best grade on my report card. Having history after math made me feel really better because I could finally put my mind on the past and get my mind off of always studying formulas, functions and the madness that comes with math so much that it could just cause a person to actually go crazy.

The best part about history was studying the countries on the map and one of the favorite things that I liked to study on the map was Europe because it had favorite countries that I now want to visit such as France, England, Italy, Ireland and Spain.

I also want to go to Hungary and tour Budapest because it just sounds really nice of a sophisticated European country. We did have a map but I didn't pass it so it wasn't a big deal anyway because I still got good grades on my report card. I couldn't wait until seventh grade ended because I just hated seventh grade. When I got on my summer break, I went to summer school and had fun and I liked it.

I went to an elementary school, played on the playground, and did some work-related activities. I think the playground helped me to revisit my childhood because in my mind it was still prevalent.

We went to a farm near the school and it was fun because we got to look at all the animals and tour the whole farm before going back to our classes. I usually made animal sounds. Even though I would be at a farm in contact with the animals, I was not allowed to bark or make animal sounds because I promised not to do it, so I didn't do it.

Author: Chelby Morgan

I didn't do that, and all went well for me because nobody had to make a report about it to her either. After a while though during my stay at summer school, I saw the same girl from my special class in third grade and she was still in the same position that she was in since fifth grade.

I mean she was still crying and throwing fits and temper tantrums and when one kid heard it, he would call her a crybaby. Now that I think about it, when I did my crying, nobody would laugh or call me a crybaby. Instead when they saw me crying in class, they would shower me with the pity party and sympathy cards by asking me if I was ok and what's wrong or don't cry.

I usually got a whole bunch of slack cut in me from other students when I started my crying and sniffling but when it came to the other girl who did almost the same thing that I did, they didn't cut her any slack. They were cruel by calling her a crybaby and laughing at and teasing her as well. That seemed very horrible to me, because I felt that she wouldn't be able to have a future for herself.

But after a while I didn't hear of her noises and fits and tantrums even though I felt really bad for her and her horrible plight as well. I trucked along in my summer school studies and it went well for me. My summer break was awesome because after summer school, I got to go to Monterrey with my whole family because we wanted to see an aquarium full of fishes.

When we went to Monterrey, we checked into a hotel called Embassy Suites and it was by far the best hotel that I've ever been to because it had connecting rooms, four beds, a pool, cable TV, free breakfast and a nice elevator that we had fun riding on.

There was a pool to go swimming in but at that time I couldn't go because it was that time of the month for me, so I didn't go. I really like swimming, but I had to wait until next time when it wasn't that time of the month for me to go swimming. The second day of our Monterey trip involved going to a carnival with plenty of rides to go on and cotton candy to try out.

I loved the days of cotton because it tasted so sweet while melting in your mouth. After a fun day at the carnival, we went to K-mart and did some bra shopping which I was excited about because I really loved to shop for bras and clothes and I was getting something new anyway, so to me there was absolute reason to be excited in someone shopping for some bras for one or three girls in the family.

On the third day, we went to a nail shop for my mom so that she could get a pedicure and a manicure, while the rest of the family got to sit in the car and be bored all day which I was. I sat in the car quietly for a while but I got bored of it eventually so I would complain about it to my dad and he told my mom about it which I didn't want to happen because she would've been happy with me trying to spoil her day. Then on the fourth day, we went to an aquarium to see fishes, water and get our pictures taken together as a family.

Author: Chelby Morgan

Then we walked around and watched people ride bikes and get in some good exercise which showed because people around me were very fit and slim without an ounce of fat in sight. We rode the bus together and we also got something good to eat before killing more time and finishing up out time to tour.

Then when it was time for us to go to bed, I would lay down to get some sleep while my brother and sister would play on the beds and laugh up a storm. Mind you they were doing it without my parents waking up and finding out about it. Next day was our last day to leave and we packed up and took pictures before we left home. I got to enjoy the rest of my summer before doing some shopping for me as far as school clothes and supplies were concerned.

Eighth grade came and I was really looking forward to it because it was about to be about being on top and getting respect. If somebody messed with me, I felt the need to handle it in a way that I saw fit to handle it. And when I did, they would start realizing that they couldn't mess with so they would be forced to respect me. This was true where in one instance one girl would mess with me and call me a derogatory name used to describe a female dog.

So I took it upon myself to hit her and bite her on the arm. She wanted to hit me back but she couldn't because my cousin told her no. Speaking of my cousins, they were my schoolmates that I would eat lunch with. I felt that it was nice to have relatives as my schoolmates and eat lunch with me to top it off.

My older cousin felt that she had to babysit because I was always jumping on the tables and walking from table to table which my aide found out about and made me stay with her for the rest of the lunch period.

She told me that if I couldn't eat like a civilized person then I didn't need to eat with my peers. So I toned it down for a bit and started eating like a civilized person. Then a few months later when I was 14, my parents informed me and my sister that we were moving to Georgia and it would take 6 to 7 days to get there because we were going to drive there.

We had a garage sale, got some things together for our road trip, said our goodbyes and left. We got to Georgia safely and my grandmother helped us get settled in our new home with a pool in the backyard and my own room and bathroom for me.

I didn't like my life in Georgia at first, but I got used to my new environment with the help of my peers and a new ParaPro who was very sweet and patient. I loved my new school and teachers as well, so I didn't have any problems with it whatsoever. One of the next hurdles that I had to get through in life was high school and that was something I was looking forward to but not really looking forward to at the same, which I will discuss in the next chapter.

CHAPTER 3

High School Was Prison

High School Was Prison

August 2005 was my first day of high school and I was really looking forward to it at first. But as time passed by I really didn't look forward to it at all. We had a small orientation before getting our schedule for classes and touring the whole school so that we as freshmen kids didn't get lost finding our classes on the first day of school.

I mean if some of us really got lost trying to find our classes on the first day of school, it probably would've been a bad day for us, but that didn't happen to me so I was good to go. One time when I was late for one class, I had to go to the attendance office to get a pass and when I did, I had detention which proved to be very stressful, but I got bailed out of it after they learned of my condition so I didn't end up having to do it at all. I got to meet my teachers on the first day of school while going over the rules and dress code at the same time.

First, I had home room before going to first period and out of nowhere I tell you, there was this boy who was tall and that was the first time I saw in real life a grill in someone's mouth. I thought that it was so cool and I wanted a grill too. I then remembered a song I memorized from this rapper from Grit Records named Derb the Knuckle head who said *"allots changed since yawl last done seen me tho, a brother done got tall and his grill is gold..."*

Author: Chelby Morgan

This boy had a gold grill and I went up to him and said "hi my name is Chelby" and I asked him was he a rapper from Grit Records? He laughed and said no and how did I know about Grit Records and that he been trying to get a record deal from there. I told him my uncle was a Boss over there.

He then surprised me and said he views me as his best friend and that he liked me very much. I didn't even know I liked grills and now I liked that boy even though he had a gold grill in his mouth.

You want to know a secret? I thought in my mind if I married that boy with the gold grill, I still would've accepted him for who he was and the way he looked. I even thought that if we were to date and he wanted to kiss me on my cheek or something, it would not have mattered that he had a grill or not. I thought he was really hot back then. Yes, even autistic teenagers do notice people who are hot.

The boy with the gold grill was cool. I remember he asked me to give him a kiss on his cheek and I was so happy. I went too far by kissing him on his cheek and that didn't go well for me, because what had happened was, I had told my uncle all about the boy at school with a gold grill and how he wanted to be a rapper for Grit Records label. My uncle said I was silly and the gold grill boy don't really like me he just want me to help him get his demo out. My uncle was right and I had not even told him about the fact that the boy with the gold grill had asked me to give my uncle his demo.

Well anyways, my uncle told my dad who in turn told my mom who then told me to come and speak to her. Word traveled fast. When my parents found out about the boy with the gold grill, they told me it wasn't right for me to kiss nobody I did not see my self getting married to.

My mom also said if I had no intentions of marrying him or he marrying me it also was not a good idea. I told her I do have intentions to marry him. She asked me did he want to marry me. I said I didn't know and that I did not ask him. She explained to me that the boy with the gold grill should be the one to ask me to marry him and if he never ask me to marry him, then that is my answer.

Well, what do you know, the boy with the gold grill never asked me to marry him. I guess it was puppy love. I wonder why they call it puppy love. I'm not a puppy. It should be called Chelby love.

One time after home room, I had economic home skills, where I was taught to cook and get along with other people. And as a class, we watched a real life movie that talked about the dangers of drinking and driving and how if you were caught drinking and driving by the law, you would really be in hot water with a serious criminal record and possibly jail, depending on how old you were at the time.

In one part of the movie it showed the dangers of drinking and driving.

There was this one teenager who hit the floor in the mall as a result of falling off an escalator because he had been drinking vodka at the time.

So that being said, he ended up in the hospital in an unconscious state of mind with no feeling in his body at all. His mom thought he would be walking when he woke up and got out of the hospital but that didn't work because he ended up being in a wheelchair for who knows how long that has been since that time.

I hope he was doing okay after that. I don't know what happened to him to this day, and only the lord knows what is going on with him right now. One girl who also saw the movie where they guy hit the floor in the mall after drinking vodka, she actually laughed at him saying that if he hadn't made that stupid decision, then he wouldn't be in that situation in the first place. I asked her to stop laughing at him and she said I was dumb and that it was not real.

The teacher overheard her and came and told her that it wasn't funny and how she agreed with me. I liked that the teacher because she sure shut her up. That girl was already getting on my nerves with her insensitivity. When the teacher had the guts to shut her up, it made a huge difference for me. Of course, drama happened with me and that girl all because of the teacher siding with me. Me and her did not get along with each other.

She was the always antagonist towards me and always sought to get to my nerves just to see me react. With that being said, I decided to get her on nerves back and see how she reacted. Well she reacted and that didn't go well for her because she got suspended and I didn't.

Her and I not getting along lasted for several months and the issue was finally resolved. She even started to be nice to me for some reason out of the blue and then I never saw her no more at the school. I guess she probably moved to another school. Cooking class was the best class ever because it involved cooking and learning about what I read from my textbook. After Home Economics, I had PE and that involved aerobics and I really enjoyed it because I liked that we could have music while doing our workout.

From my point of view there is nothing wrong with me. But in high school, my peers said I talked and sounded funny and made strange noises, faces and was very loud. I told them I was one of them for the most part and that they were mistaken. I did meet a few people who were very nice in welcoming me into their group. I felt that they weren't going to judge me for the way I may have looked, dressed sounded and or just being different in general.

When I talked, they listened and even told me that's not how things are and they even would help me understand why not. They in turn told me about their experiences and about having mean teachers in middle school.

Author: Chelby Morgan

They told me what they would've done if their teachers were like some of mine were. To pass time I liked listening to R&B, Country and even Rap music. I would write down the lyrics to my favorite songs that I could sing to my classmates.

My good friend who was a class mates gave me the idea to stand up in front of the class right before we got started and to sing out in front of the class as a surprise to the teacher and the rest of my classmates and show off my talents to everyone. So I did that. And everyone was laughing and smiling and I was so happy. The teacher yelled at me at first and then she started to clap and then everyone clapped.

It was like a concert for me. After class my teacher said that I should not sing in front of the class anymore and save my talents for the stage. I asked her where was the stage at and when should I go there because now I wanted to be a singer and rapper and write my own rap lyrics and sing to all of my schoolmates at the entire school.

She said that first I had to graduate school and to focus on that. I told my friend who expressed a desire to hear more. So from that point on I decided to write some lyrics and I told her I could sing to my classmates at lunch time. I thought it turned out pretty good because they really liked it. At lunch time everyone started to ask me to sing songs for them and they would all laugh and dance around me and say "go Chelby, go Chelby."

Once I rapped about hitting the ones who bullied me with a bottle. I used the lyrics I heard on the radio. This one girl said I stole that song from somebody on the radio.

But like the rest of the other kids they decided to hear me anyway and seemed to have a little bit of understanding of what I was going through with the kid bullying me about me being so-called retarded and handicapped. I really got some of the bullies real good one time, which will be discussed later.

What else? After aerobics, I had language arts with a teacher who was really good at what she taught, had patience and didn't put up with nonsense either. In the class, I soon found another boy that I had a crush on. He didn't have a gold grill in his mouth and his mouth was normal. Guess what. Before I even took a liking to him, I threw my pencil and eraser at him and marked him up.

I had to stop marking on him and was told I would have serious consequences if I didn't stop. I did stop all that but I really had a crush on him and I thought he was really cute to begin with. I even started writing secret letters to him and calling him a beautiful person. I knew of other teenagers who would openly tell their parents about the crushes that they had on the opposite sex but that wasn't the case with me because It also felt kinda awkward to tell them that. I felt they wouldn't understand so I didn't tell them that part.

Somehow my mom found about it. I don't know how she knew, but she always seemed to know stuff. Anyway, we had a good conversation about it even though I wasn't always in a good disposition to talk about it. If you are wondering where I get my big words from it is in the dictionary and I know what they mean.

Back to my story, even as a wild child and typical teenager, I always felt my mom had my best interest at heart. Once she told me that she wanted me to have a suitable man that would love me from the heart and not abuse me. I told my mom getting abused wasn't an option and I was not going to stand for that. On the other hand, though I wanted to be with guys that were cool and I liked rappers and singer types.

The rappers were what all the girls seemed to talk about so that was my type as a teenager. I really didn't understand and was glad to have parents who did. I thought rappers were cool but I never thought that I would encounter a wife beater for that matter. Mom also told me that if she found out that I found someone I could love, to let her know. I told her about this rapper I liked and later found out his songs sang about beating on women.

She said that the rapper would not have told me that he beat women if he was really the type to marry. I may have married him though at that time but I'm now super glad it never happened. She told me all about sex and to be careful and how everyone could take advantage of me.

I heard from other girls at school, how some girls in high school were in the bathroom stalls and would end up pregnant by the time they left the bathroom stalls.

Well it turns out that the rapper I liked left another girl and she ended up with STD. I'm so glad I listened to my parents because I was not about that life. I was sure that it could happen to me if I was in the same situation because was not invincible.

Looking back with that attitude I had, it showed how young and naive I was because I felt that I was invincible to consequences to certain behavior. I felt that being young meant not having to think about or accept the consequences. I wanted to have fun while I could. I didn't want to wait until I got older to learn more about life, I wanted everything now. Now in my mind I wanted to be a rappers girlfriend like the other girls. I wanted lotsa friends like all the other girls had. Even tho I tried to be their friends some just laughed at me. But I still held out some hope that someday a rapper or singer would come and surprise me with a relationship as a my boyfriend.

I wasn't being a pest but he left for another school after telling another girl that he wanted as a girlfriend that he was leaving her for another school with her telling him "forget you then." After he left I decided to keep trying in pursuing somebody as a true boyfriend that would love me and make me feel loved and safe in a relationship. Again, this was part of me not understanding life, love and autism.

Author: Chelby Morgan

Well when it was lunchtime, we would form a line to get the best food that the south had to offer.

Then we finished the rest of language arts before going to our last period for the day. The last period that I had was PE where once I was sitting alone on the bleachers talking to myself before some girls approached me and asked me who I was talking to and what I was doing.

They befriended me and gently told me not to talk to myself so other people would not talk about me or laugh at me. They asked me to sing some songs for them and showed me some dance moves to do. I thought the moves were lewd and told them that but at the same time it did seem cute to me. Once I did the dance before class and then this one boy ask me to go out with him and that he would pick me up from my house.

He asked for my address and I gave it to him so that he would come to my house and pick me up for a date. My parents didn't approve, and they didn't find out about it until later on in life because I was not about to tell them about my date who was coming to my house to pick me up. If I did, they might have said no.

Well even tho he said that he would pick me up from my house, he really didn't come at all.

So, it gave me plenty of time to write him a love letter and talk to him like I would a best friend before letting them find out about our personal relationship. He never seemed to want to come to my house but he always asked me to go out with him.

A few times before I said yes, I would meet him he would say to stay home if I don't want to go out with him. Part of me was like "forget you" since he stood me up many times. Thats what Ceeloo Green said in a song. Anyway I wouldn't go out with him not because I didn't want to go out with but I was done being stood up and the other reasons was I sort of felt I wasn't allowed to go on dates with boys.

I never wanted to tell him that because he may have gotten a bad opinion about me from that point on. You know as a teenager who was going through a lot of changes and brain morphing along with hormonal issues, the opinions from my classmates really mattered to me to the point where I would do anything to fit in and be liked by them.

Being autistic had its own unique issues. You want to fit in and try your best to do what you think the girls your age is doing. But for me, my emotions were all over the place.

To be honest, if it had not been for the love of my parents, and teachers and true friends, I don't know how I would have made it out of high school.

I could have gotten tricked into doing something very bad and it would have been disastrous for me. One boy I liked even robbed Bank of America and if I would have been his girlfriend, I guess I would have been a bank robber to. I wondered if I would have had to wear a mask. It gets stuffy in there.

Well, needless to say, the boy I liked who led me on, he moved onto another girl despite having interest in me. After time he was always trying to be in my face talking about how he hadn't seen me in a long time even though he was the one who helped in getting me excluded from a group of kids that he and I were part of at the time all because some girls didn't want me in their group at all.

I really thought they were my friends but turns out they were the ones who encouraged some kids to beat me up. Ohh yeah mom if you a readying this part in my book I never told you guys this part because I felt that the situation would've been worse to begin with so I kept it to myself because there was this one girl that I wanted to get rid of who was making fun of me and she talked bad about my hair, and called me fat and retarded and big headed.

I challenged her to a fist fight and I told my classmates about it but they discouraged me from doing it because they said I would've been in more trouble. Of course that plan didn't happen and the same girl who was making fun of me and calling me names calmed that down because a teacher had said something to her about it and probably told her that if she didn't stop then she would be in trouble.

Over time that girl began to be nice to me until she left for another school. I thought I was going to miss her but it turned out that I didn't miss her at all. Then there was another boy who kept asking me for dates and would talk about how he ain't seen me in a long time.

That boy would start some small talk with me which I accepted because I really wanted somebody to talk to. It seemed less and less people would talk to me and only noticed my abilities or disabilities if you will. I wanted anyone to say something to make me feel better. With my autism, many times I always felt confused and alone. Even though I had my family I still felt alone.

My mind understood that I had my family, but I still felt a void. Like something was missing. Now by this time I knew how boys was being all fake because the ones that said they liked me, really didn't care about me to begin with. After all, even with autism, I realized he was just a "boy." from what I saw, all boys wanted was a good time with girls.

My parents had not approved of going on dates and it really worked out well for me and my best interests. I had come to the point I no longer felt need for somebody to be in my face telling me sweet nothings. Then one time during my home room class, I saw this other guy that I kinda liked, but he didn't return that feeling back to me.

In fact he told me that don't nobody like my ugly behind (he used the a word)

Author: Chelby Morgan

When he said that it made me mad to the point where I started to write some derogatory words about him on the desk. The teacher found out about it and sent me to the office with the assistant principal punishing me with ISS which stands for IN SCHOOL SUSPENSION.

I had that punishment for three days and had to pick up garbage. I would sing rap songs and do "laffy taffy" dances that some kids encouraged me to do. I did what they encouraged me to do because I had planned on being an entertainer and make people happy.

A big part of me felt that I did allot of things to be accepted socially. At the time I did not realize that I was injuring my own reputation, and my self. After a few days of being out of ISS, I was assigned another ParaPro to help me through high school and to help me manage my social behavior.

I hated it because I now felt that I wouldn't be a normal teenager with normal friends because they would just walk away from me and think that I was weird with a ParaPro. So I felt that when I was 18, I was going to move out and get my own place so that I could do my own thing and come and go about the world as I please.

Some people may not understand about people with autism is that, we still have feelings and emotions like everyone else. Having autism means I do not know where to interject certain feelings and behaviors and other things out of place.

I didn't like the idea of having a Para Pro following me around everywhere I went, because of what it would look like for a teenager who was trying to blend in with the rest of the regular teenagers, who were already regular teenagers, with regular teenage issues to begin with.

Now I got a agent following me and making sure I don't get into things. I gave my para pro a hard time and pretended like she was following me around. I would tell everyone who is she. I kept giving her a hard time and would act up and say she isn't my para pro to begin with. Now I had an extra body following me around telling me what was right and wrong about everything I did.

I already had parents and teachers and family already doing that for me. So that being said, one time when I had a computer class where I had to type up paragraphs and letters, I was always behind because I couldn't type that fast and everyone around me was very proficient at typing as well.

I hated that class, and I mocked the teacher because the classroom was loathsome not to mention my Para pro kept telling me to stop doing whatever I was doing. I didn't listen because I didn't like being managed or told what to do.

When I mocked the teacher and my parents found out about it, they put me on restrictions and made me apologize to the teacher which I felt like I didn't have to.

Author: Chelby Morgan

I thought if you are not sorry you don't apologize. Since I really wasn't sorry why apologize at all for she was only there to make my life miserable as far as I was concerned.

The only thing that got me through the class was some students who were fun and enjoyed my sense of humor.

I started to enjoy how my classmates talked to teachers, how they dressed and because they did things a little bit more funner then me or what adults wanted children to be at the time. Being autistic means I see the world differently. My brain is wired differently .

Once I got to do a slideshow about our childhood, choice of music and entertainment, dress, hobbies and much which I got a B on because the teacher liked my slideshow. She was a strict teacher but as time passed by I started to like her, even though I couldn't wait to get out of that class for it was too hard for me.

Besides, I didn't think I would even need it after I graduated from high school because my plan was to be a rapper or singer and they wouldn't need to use a computer anyway. All a rapper and singer needs to do is be recorded while they rap or sing their songs and their producers and managers will take care of the rest.

Anyway, my freshmen year could've been better but I was glad that freshmen year was over with because I hated being on the bottom of the totem pole as it were. I hoped that my sophomore year would be better come to find out I hated that as well.

My sophomore year came but there was nothing likeable or exciting about except for when I had drama, my favorite classes such as English and history, a girl who seemed to like me like my family helped me to escape. One of the class that I had was drama and I enjoyed that very much because I could by myself and really be in the zone.

Drama helped me maintain and kept me in the TV zone with a focus on being an actress when I grew up. In fact, drama was something I wanted to pursue in college because that's something that I enjoyed doing. Twice we had a play for the whole school to see and it went really nice because the whole school liked it.

Another class that I had was algebra which I hated to death because it would be hard and I was always behind without the help of the teacher because the teacher was obviously handcuffed to the curriculum. I was left on my own while some others succeeded with almost no effort. So hating math class I decided to give the teacher some problems by mocking him a bit and doing other things to even give my ParaPro problems.

It was to the point where she had take me to the principal's office for a time-out and I got a lecture from the principal. At times I thought, I'd rather be at the principal's office than be in that algebra class but only if my parents didn't know about it of course.

If I could go there, I'd be to just sit there and think about everything that I've done. I didn't get a good grade for that class but I got transferred to another class that dealt with the concepts of algebra which I thought was nice because the teacher explained it in more details and was even nice to me as well.

The funny thing is, even in the next grade I struggled to fit in and had the desire to fit in and be the most popular student at the school.

I even resolved in my mind that I would do whatever it took to earn the status and was going to form a gang and be the leader with tattoos and piercings, and wear gangster clothes, and then would have friends from the hood to hang out with, and maybe even go to nightclubs and parties, like on TV and just hang out with and don't do algebra.

On TV people from the hood and the projects don't seem to do no algebra. All they do is bully other people and they get respect and are cool and popular.

But of course, I never did those things, but it did cross my mind to do them if that means I can fit in as my brain was sorta encouraging me to do. I no some other kids with autism and all they do is yell scream cruse all day long and throw fits. One boy punches his dad in the face and runs real fast.

I wanted to do all those things but my mom never let me do that. My uncle even said "aint nothing wrong with you so if you act up you will deal with the consequences of acting up even with autism." He then asked me did I want to bite or hit him. I said yes. He said I could, but he would do whatever I did to him to me. I said I don't want him to bite or hit me. He said then don't bite or hit him. He also said in the Hebrew scriptures it was called an eye for an eye.

I started to understand with autism, you don't always rationalize the consequences. You just do whatever comes to your mind. In my mind all I wanted to do was fit in any way I could.

One time I wrote down all of my life plans in a secret diary that apparently was not a secret because my mom found out about it and I had to talk about it.

I felt that she just wouldn't understand me as a real teenage human being with real teenage struggles to fit in and just enjoy being a teenager for that matter. We resolved my life plans and she told me to just be myself and people will like my personality.

I moved on to other things. The law said if you were 15, you had to have a permit to be taught how to drive. If you were learning how to drive you had to drive with your parents before getting your license at 16. I wanted to make that my goal but it didn't happen at the time and I was feeling sorry for myself. I felt that I wouldn't be able to have the same freedoms that some teenagers had.

One prime example of that was when one girl in class was learning to drive at 15 before getting her license at 16 because when everything "fell in place for her", I was really wishing to switch lives with her. I felt that her life was more better than mine.

And in my mind she was very pretty with makeup and the nice clothes to top it off because she always felt comfortable in her own skin without caring too much about what people thought about her. I on the other hand didn't always think that I was pretty so I thought that makeup would cover up my flaws so that I could be pretty.

Only later did I realize that I was loved and had a distorted view of love because I was still a kid at that time. I wasn't allowed to wear make-up but I still felt bad about the way I looked and would often compare myself to some other girls who I felt looked better than me, especially when they wore makeup and had nicer clothes and shoes to top it off.

In my mind, they even had perfect bodies that they didn't even worry about because they were always about being thin and keeping their bodies filled with "diet food" such as salads and baked chicken, not fried. I loved fried chicken more than baked.

At one point, I wanted to be thin so bad that if I would just stop eating certain foods or just not eat at all, then I would be successful at being thin. Once I even thought that either my death would be better for me because there was this one girl that I was jealous of.

I felt she was upstaging me and making me not feel comfortable about the way I looked sounded and spoke. By this time I realized I was different and that she was not laughing with me more or less at me. I hated her to the point of not even talking to her and wanted her to never get ice cream again. I never said anything to her about how I felt but now that I think about it, I was really being ugly towards her because my jealousy really got to me.

I felt that she was getting more attention. Well anyone would get attention by the way she looked and dressed, and that made me jealous. I even felt left out and I just didn't want anything to do with her. I now look upon that with regret and wish that I just reached out to her.

If your reading this Adriana I really apologize to you for the way I was back then. I was just jealous and acting ugly toward you. It wasn't right for me to do that to you. You are more than welcomed to reach out to me and give me a call.

Well we left Georgia in 2007 which I thought I would miss because I was just getting used to my environment and I just didn't want to go to California, so I thought that I would live with my grandmother until graduation and I would move into an apartment in Georgia so that I could be close to the 4 friends I made from school and pursue my rapping, modeling and acting career in Atlanta. I mean Hotlanta.

I felt that it wouldn't happen because I didn't have a job to help me move to Georgia and pursue my career in those fields. I along with my family lived with my aunt and uncle and I really did not want to leave Georgia because I was starting my junior year at a high school. I was getting used to that and with that being said I felt that I had to be popular.

I heard it was a honor of being a junior who was considered top dog as juniors. But then I began to have a change of heart after learning about being in independent studies. Turns out I loved it and it was better for me, because I came to a conclusion that I wouldn't have to be pressured into doing homework that was due the next day and guess what, I came to a conclusion that independent studies was a great relief for me.

Another great relief for me was being able to comprehend and study subjects at my own pace without having to take tests every week. So I looked forward to learning every time I woke up from my bed.

I put my former dream careers on hold because I first wanted to stay at home with my parents for a very long time but as time passed by I voiced my desire to move out, pursue my careers and finally get some freedom. I didn't start thinking about those things yet, because I was immersed in my studies at my independent studies' program and the nice teacher that I had for my studies.

I really enjoyed doing independent studies because I liked the classes that I was taking and the good grades that I got from the help of my teacher. She was just awesome because she was always willing to take the time and effort to tutor me and help me pass my test for math which I did because that was a nice gateway for me to graduate from high school which I desperately wanted to do all along because I wanted high school to be history.

I was so waiting to be out of high school so that I could really get on with my life and find a job. But as time passed and fall came, I went back to listening to R&B and Rap music and watching videos to the point where it sparked my interest in pursuing a career in the music, acting and comedy industry because I really liked to entertain and make people laugh.

Plus I felt bored with the life that I had at home and desired more that life in the music and entertainment industry had to offer. I thought: Look at what the entertainment industry has to offer: frequent traveling to places that you want to go to, big houses, nice cars, complete freedom, and all kinds of accolades that most people would dream to have.

I also wanted to have whatever I liked such as designer clothes, jewelry, shoes, makeup, and all other things that I felt like I wasn't getting at home so I decided to make some serious plans to move out and pursue those goals that I felt would get further into happiness, fame, wealth and fortune. I decided that when I was 18 and had already graduated from high school, I would move to Atlanta, go to Spellman college for acting, be a comedian and pursue a career in rapping or singing.

First I was going to have a garage sale to pay for my airplane ticket to Atlanta, get a job, have my own apartment, and finally go about my business in the entertainment world.

Of course that didn't happen because I had to put that on the back burner for I needed help in finding a place, filling out certain applications and having my progress monitored before I could move to Atlanta.

I felt like I had a thing going for me that I felt that I just didn't need somebody helping me because I really wanted to just to be out of state and have my own space and freedom. We were looking for an apartment for me but as time went by I decided to stay at home and pursue another career because I could really see how hard life would be in the real world with real bills, a full-time job, more responsibilities and people that wouldn't just care about you or have your best interests at heart because some of them would only want to help with something in return for their generosity.

Staying at home really worked out well for me because I was able to really help my parents out around the house, get along with them more, and just really see what I needed to work on as far as my attitude and mental disposition was concerned.

I was even able to enjoy the house that I was living in because it was beautiful with good neighbors, a park and a quiet neighborhood to top it off. Now that I think about it, I was just such a mess without the word "hot" included in it because I had so much things to work on that it just wasn't even funny.

One of them being was that being patient was not one of my strongest points in my younger years, because with me I was always looking for quick fast and in a hurry kind of solutions and conveniences. My thing was that I did not feel like waiting for anything, I just wanted them now when I wanted them to be.

I was just a mess that needed a lot of working on and if I didn't work on it and I just sought immediate conveniences and solutions and relief then I would be in trouble right now. I liked being older because I couldn't wait to get out of high school so graduation here I came.

CHAPTER 4

Graduation At Last

Graduation At Last

Guess what? Graduation finally came around the corner on June 2009. Funny thing, my grandmother was also graduating from a 4 year college that same year getting her Masters.

I was glad to graduate from high school because I was waiting to finally be done with high school and all the drama that had come with it. Graduation was my day for me to get a little spoiled. For my graduation I got a shopping spree, hair pampering, spa pampering, a new cell phone, a more gifts. I also got dinner after my graduation ceremony.

I did not complain about any of them all because I felt that I earned them through hard work, perseverance, and diligence so I kept myself thankful and did not expect much. First off, I went to the spa on Gateway Blvd to get a facial and a threading. I wanted to look decent for both my ceremony and pictures that would be taken afterwards. The Green Valley Spa was great when I got my facial. After a while it did start to hurt so I had to stop the session because it got too hurt to much for me.

At least my face was clean and presentable, so I didn't ask for much in the end. For the threading though it started to hurt but I pushed through it until I decided not to go there anymore because they started to hurt too much which I don't regret because the pain from it is not there anymore.

Author: Chelby Morgan

I traded that in for a brow waxing job because it doesn't hurt as much, even though I don't always go there either because I just don't feel like it. Then a few days later I had to attend my ceremony.

I went to a salon in Vacaville and got my hair cut, washed and flat ironed and I really liked it because she did a fabulous job on it, like she always does now because I now currently go there for I know she will do a wonderful job while offering a fair and reasonable price for her service.

When that was being said and done, my mom and I went to do some shopping at Sacs for some new clothes to wear. The clothes that we stumbled upon were a dressy blouse, nice capri pants, earrings, necklace, a bracelet, and some shoes. I first wanted some heels, but was convinced otherwise so I didn't press the issue.

Then when we got home, we had to get ready for the ceremony because it started at three and we had to make sure we were going in the right direction because this would be our first time going on J street in Sacramento.

Before driving on the freeway to Sacramento, we headed to pick up my dad from his place of work before picking up a friend that I invited to come along for the ride. After that, we headed off to Sacramento and begin the journey. Once we got there we parked and got situated while my mom got the camera together so she could take pictures and videotape me.

I went inside with my graduating class so that we could walk in and get our diplomas from the stage. While waiting to obtain our diplomas, some girls were complaining about their feet hurting as a result of wearing high heels but one of the teachers told her that if she wasn't wearing heels, her feet wouldn't be hurting. I was then glad I didn't wear any heels because I had a lot of freedom to walk around on stage without the worry of slipping and falling on stage.

My mom had tears of joy when she saw me on stage taking the diploma and then when the ceremony was over, we went out to dinner. The place that we went to was called Joes Crab Shack and the sky was the limit for me so I was able to order what I wanted. I ordered some fried coconut fish with some fries and a soda.

My mom tried some of my fried coconut fish and they were delicious that she should've got the same thing that I had so that we could be twins and she could benefit from it tasting good. I don't remember what she ordered but I know my dad had a lobster bucket with some potatoes.

I now wish I had lobster but I didn't order it at the time because I didn't think I would like it. I think that I should have ordered it because, one of these days later on, I was able to taste it and I liked it enough to have it for lunch and dinner.

I wanted to get some dessert but I don't remember if I ordered desert. But I know I had a good time. I also had a good day because I was able to put high school behind me, and focus on my day and evening. I now would spend more time with my family and friends, and plan for my future.

Then after a few days of going to Joes Crab Shack, my family planned a week for me to go to Great America in Santa Rosa so we got packed up, booked a hotel, and headed off to Santa Rosa with My Uncle and young cousins in tow.

Before heading off on the freeway, we went to Vallejo to get gas but while that was happening, I had to go to the bathroom and before I was done, there was not enough toilet paper and only no soap. I found sanitizer in my purse and washed my hands with hot water. I vowed never to go that gas station again.

Then when we got to Santa Rosa, we checked into a hotel called Hawthorne Suites and got a nice package for our trip to Great America which was wonderful because it offered a really big fat discount on our whole tickets and souvenirs.

That hotel that we stayed at was very wonderful and to my liking because it had a pull-out sofa for me to sleep on just in case I wanted to sleep in my own bed instead of sharing a bed with my sister.

It worked out well because I didn't always have to sleep in the same with somebody else so I was really being spoiled at that time.

The first time that we went to Great America, I got to get on some cool rides minus the rides that were very scary and uncomfortable.

Then because I got an American Express card, I got to spend some money on some souvenirs shops and come out with some necklaces and key chains.

Then there was another shop that sold some belts and shirts which I wanted to get but then I remembered that we had some shops that we could get those things at back in town so I passed them up eventually. Then one night after going to Great America, we went to KFC to get some food for dinner and what we had was Cole slaw, chicken and potatoes.

I preferred mashed because they always serve that instead of baked or boiled for that matter. I didn't want to get any Cole slaw because I really didn't care for it but I ended up getting it anyway because it was supposedly part of the meal.

Then on our last day, we went to Great America before heading home. Then days after going to Great America, I attended my cousin's graduation party at my uncle's house and her friends were there to support her and celebrate their own graduations as well.

CHAPTER 5

Welcome To Adulthood

Welcome To Adulthood

Its now after graduation. I was now a semi-unconventional person who would now play by the so-called rules of adults and how adults are supposed to act. If I bark and laugh as an adult, I figure no one will call me retard or judge me on it.

I previously learned that, as a child you must listen to adults and now that I am considered an adult, I wondered if it would be the same for me? Will things be different? I woke up today and feel I am into fashion so I went to a store called Ross. I would shop for cute shirts. There were some skirts there, but I didn't get around to looking at them close enough to buy them.

When I got out of the store though, I was wishing that I did look at them a little more. Ross was always my store because they had cheap stuff that was sometimes name brand and really cute and fashionable.

I loved shopping at Ross and had been shopping there for years. I'm sorry Ross if you are reading this, but I also fell in love with another store called JC Penny which I will talk about in a little while.

Anyway, while I was still living at my parents' house, my cousin Yana came to live in town with my aunt and uncle and she got settled into her nice bedroom with her own bathroom.

When I heard of the news, I was really excited because now I could see my cousin whenever my heart desired. Believe you me, I loved my cousin so much, that I wanted to do stuff together with her like shopping and going to this interesting restaurant she would go to called Black Bear Diner.

I heard all about Black Bear Diner from my cousin who went in there to get some fries. Its been a while but I cant remember much about going there. It wouldn't hurt for me to ask around because I just don't remember going there allot.

Ever since hearing about that restaurant, I had been wanting to go there, so I started asking my other family members if we could all go there. We had not got around to it. Sooner or later we will all go there. I want to go there because I hear that their food is delicious especially the mashed potatoes and steak along with some corn and gravy. I like corn.

They also have specials where kids would eat free meals on a Tuesday. Problem is, I am not a kid anymore so I don't qualify. The way I understand it, any kid who goes there on a Tuesday gets to eat a free meal. Wow, that is good and most fortunate for kids because they get to eat for free with no cost or any hard work that goes into paying for the meal.

When your young kids can mow lawns, clean their room or house and do odd jobs for extra money while living at home free of bills and rent.

Of course, I live at home rent free and I didn't have to pay bills. I thought that since I am an adult I should apply for a job and I applied everywhere. I went to Big Lots who was hiring. Even though they said they were hiring they never would hire me or let me do an interview for some reason. Since I never heard back from them, I applied for other jobs somewhere else.

That being said I relied on my parents to give me money as a monthly allowance. This was until I could get a job or a monthly stipend elsewhere. I did really good with the allowance because it allowed me to buy some toiletries and do some light shopping at places like Ross and even Big Lots on a debit card that I obtained when I was 18.

One thing that I had to do all the time was get my eyebrows threaded at a Green Valley Spa on Gateway Blvd. I liked getting that done a few times but when I had to do that every month it started to be something that I just wasn't always looking forward to because of the pain that came with the threading.

I wanted to get a brow waxing there but it was expensive, so I had to go for the threading because it was only $8.00. I had been getting the threading done to my eyebrows until I heard that you could get a waxing on Sunset Avenue for $10.00 from my aunt, so I decided to abandon the threading altogether and go for a waxing until I stopped doing that waxing as well because they really hurt.

I would get my brows done but they would have to not hurt at all. That's the thing and I have yet to get around to it anyway so it'll be awhile until I can deal with it.

Now the guys started to notice me more and the older I got, the more I started to feel vulnerable especially because of how guys would start looking at me and hollering at me and saying things like Hey sexy... its bad enough I have disabilities and hard enough to hide my appearance or expressions that may give it away that I have issues, but at the same time I am not really looking for attention like that from guys.

I just want to go about my business without all the unwanted attention all on me. There was an ad that was eye-catching from men looking for hot babes only. When I saw that, I thought that It didn't apply to me because I'm not a hot babe and my temperature is always constant.

Then I found out from my family that a hot babe was meant other things. From what I understand the definition of a hot babe is someone that dresses really nice and has flawless with makeup and appearance. No one can possibly be a hot babe since no one is perfect and everyone has flaws in some manner. A hot babe also could not be me because I totally don't think I fit that qualification.

I would say im kinda hot. I thought, if a guy wants a hot babe he might be weird or is superficial and is asking for nothing but disappointments.

If I had to get my eyebrows done monthly and look all hot, I can imagine what hot babes have to do. I also would be mad if a guy is staring at me just because he thinks I'm a hot looking babe. So that being said when I was 18, I wasn't about wearing mini-skirts or daisy dukes because I wanted to keep myself covered up.

I decided to dress more on the conservative side. At times I would wear tank tops, but I never wanted to wear certain tank tops out in public because I didn't want anything exposed or tempting for a guy. Because of my disabilities and issues that come with my disabilities, I decided to keep my hot babeness to myself and would not wear skintight clothes despite allot of girls who wore extra skin tight jeans.

It is also easy when you don't have anyone to impress not to follow fads or the norms. So not wearing skintight jeans wasn't the end of the world for me. Just for fun I tried some on at home to see what all the fuss is about.

To me wearing tight jeans was not for me because when you wear them, they're not comfortable to begin with it shows all of your assets if you no what I mean. Even wearing daisy dukes were not an option because they too were short and tight and it just didn't fit well with me.

Don't get me wrong, I still am about fashion because I am seen shopping at stores like Ross and Big Lots JCPenney's. I even shot at Costco to obtain some clothes they even have for good bargains.

Author: Chelby Morgan

I enjoy living at home because there was a park for me to play at and to walk around on and I have a good time. Whenever I went to the park, I would get on my gym shoes and walk across the street to the park and walk around a path until I was ready to go home.

Sometimes after my walk, I would stay behind and play on the swings until it either got dark or I was ready to go home. Then my mom felt that it wasn't safe for me to go by myself, so I was stuck until I could get one of my brothers or sisters to come walk with me.

At first, that didn't sit well for me because I was used to walking by myself and would come back when I felt like coming back. But now when one of my siblings wanted to go home, I had to go home when they felt like going home.

I sorta didn't like that and felt like a prisoner because now I still didn't freedom to go wherever I wanted, whenever I wanted to go. To me, it didn't seem fair. Later I understood the reason will take advantage of me and even could snatch me up just for being by myself.

There was a girl younger then me found dead in the park and left naked and the killer was lurking in the area! Even thou I hear about things like that I felt it shouldn't happen to me because I dint do anything and felt that living in a quiet neighborhood reduces the chances of people wanting to do harm to me.

Back then I thought the chances were slim and there would be witnesses around to look out for me and rat out the one that may have tried to harm me.

I was careful with keeping the doors locked. We had a garage door that led to the backyard and if I didn't lock it especially when I was about to leave, someone would be able to walk in the garage and just steal stuff like my dad's tools.

And when my parents were going somewhere, and when they left the garage door open one of us kids would sit out in the garage to protect the stuff. I figured since they left it opened they probably were gonna come back with some heavy stuff that required some accommodation to put it that way.

So that being said, and also, when my parents were about to leave and they happen to leave they would have either me or my siblings sit out in the garage to watch the tools so that nobody would be able to steal because when you think about it, people who steal tools will either keep to themselves or sell them for some money.

I was just thinking about that when I was in a really questionable neighborhood and there would be a yard guy at someone's house to do them service. Well while he was doing that, he had all his yard tools locked up really secure so that no one would steal them.

Then that started to make sense. I remember thinking about a news article I read about housekeepers working in a New York hotel and what they had to go through on the job. This man had a dog in his hotel room and when the housekeeper came in to clean, the dog had tore in her leg while the owner stole the housekeepers broom.

Author: Chelby Morgan

Now the house keeper walks with a limp for the rest of her life all because the nerves in her legs had been permanently damaged. That really made me mad because I felt that it wasn't fair for her to have to go walking around with a limp while the owner evidently got away with it and her broom.

If I were her, I would have been filing a gabillion dollar lawsuit against him. My limp would be proof that I deserve to be compensated me for my injuries and damages. I would have felt that as a housekeeper I was in there to do a job and get it done but when the dog came along and tore up my leg, the owner who got away with it should be the one to pay for my messed up leg.

From that point on, and needles to say, I felt that I wouldn't be able to work as a housekeeper because of that bad impression that I had formed against that industry. Then again I might be able to work in the industry because some hotels don't allow pets in the rooms.

If there happen to be a pet in the hotel room and I got attacked, I would be ready to file a lawsuit against the owner because I would want to be compensated for my injuries.

I still will be doing it down to this day. Anyways at our last house, sometimes I would be lazy with keeping the doors locked but now I think that I'm cracking down a bit on security because the last thing that I want is somebody that I don't know being in my house ready to harm me or kill me.

There's never been any good news on CNN that I could use, so I don't watch the news much. I used to have a friend in Sacramento but that friendship wasn't working out for either of us.

With me friends are supposed to last forever. When I get up from my bed I do my utmost to keep all of my friends as much as I possibly can because I don't want to lose not one of them anytime soon. To me, friends should be like family and are somebody that looks out for their friends and has their best interests at heart.

They also do stuff together like hang out at your house, go to a movie and do lots of cool things together. Things started to open up for me because through my mother, I happen to have a great aunt who I remember only knowing when I was a baby so I asked for number and address along with an email so I could call her and even send her some letters at that.

I do most calls on the phone with her because I found that when I tried to send her emails she doesn't even get them so I felt that it would be better to just call her and hear her voice. I really enjoy talking to her because one time she told me about a dairy farm in Wisconsin that had cheese and milk.

Well that being said I wanted to go to Illinois to visit her and see the dairy farm in Wisconsin and try out their cheese and milk. Ohh yeah, the thing was I would have to take some Beano to control my gas because I am lactose intolerant.

For a while I had it bad but then right now I just stopped taking it. I still have her number, but I don't always get a chance to speak with her. Then before the year came to an end, a case worker was assigned to me in helping me find a job but before doing that, she proceeded to review my case and work on goals as far as what I wanted to do for a job and what kind of school that I desired to attend to fit my job goals.

Also before she even stepped foot into my house, I had been in the process of clipping my toenails so short that some of them started to bleed so I had to put tissue on them before she even got here. While we were going over some goals for jobs I was thinking about all the secretarial work that I could do in the future but it didn't dawn in me until 19 years of age where I decided that I wanted to do book writing and start a business at that as well.

I didn't get around to it until now where I truly know what I want to do which is to set up website for autistic adults and start a business at that as well. So I have now to put it together and start on it now.

I also remember there was a special occasion that came up where one of my friends graduated from high school and her parents held a graduation party for her at her their house in Suisun. I went to the party but didn't deliver a gift to her because I forgot. We were already struggling to get directions to her house at the last minute from someone that had already been there and that's why I forgot.

We kept calling her phone until she answered and gave us all directions because if we didn't have it at all, we would've gave up and went home. We did go and have a good time but the rest of my family left and I got to stay behind as long as somebody was able to give me a ride back home.

We stayed for a long time and had a ball because we played a few songs such as Bad Romance by Lady Gaga. I really liked that song and I still do down to this day because she spoke some French in her song. I figure if I keep playing it over and over again, I will be able to listen to French all day long because that's what I'm into right now.

Besides, it reminds me of sophistication when I think of France because they speak the language so sophisticated without any slipups. The french language they speak sounds neat. One day I might learn French and totally immerse myself into the language and culture because it seems sophisticated.

During the summer, we had a picnic at the park near my house when we had invited a few friends over for some hot dogs and hamburgers. There was tennis and baseball involved as activities but since I didn't think that they people who came wanted to play with me or that it wouldn't be interesting enough I decided to go do some walking around the park for a bit.

I played on the playground and I started barking. I don't know why I bark at times but I seem to bark.

Author: Chelby Morgan

When I went back home to the party I barked at the party and people was wondering how I was so good at barking and then one girl said that I really sounded like a dog.

Oh and speaking of sounding like a dog, I even know how to sound like a chihuahua without even doing a whole bunch of trying. Some people said that I am so good at sounding like a dog that it annoys them and not to do it. I can also bark and do a little howling as well.

The reason I bark is if somebody banged at the door and try to break in, I would hide in my room and lock the door before and do my barking so much that they would think that there is a dog at home and would then leave the premises right away. I think that if I could do my barking for an acting job as a test, I would probably pass because I am just that good at sounding like a dog. I always put on a big smile and that's what everyone would see all the time because I really enjoyed life and their company as well.

Now around the beginning of 2010 for some reason, I started being obsessed with counting calories and being thin. It went on until I was about 20 and then I was just no longer worried about having to count calories or even starving myself during snack time, because I really didn't want to eat any snacks before dinnertime because I felt that they would make me look fat.

That thinking all stemmed back to when I was a little chunky in high school and I was still obsessed with being like some of the girls who were thin with nice clothes, shoes and makeup. I did think about how thin and pretty I wanted to be in school sometimes and how I wanted to be liked by everyone.

But then again and most importantly, I wanted to be healthy and didn't feel any motivation until long after I got out of high school. When I was a teen I almost got obsessed about being thin and wanted to block out the voice that I felt told me that I wasn't pretty enough to even to be liked or accepted for the way I looked. Now that I think about it, to block it all out, I would begin counting calories and working out a lot because in my mind to be thin, I would have to work out a lot to reach that kind of goal.

So now I begin checking out workout DVDs that would encourage me to work all the parts of my body especially my abs because that's the part of my body that I just wanted flat so that I wouldn't have to deal with any flab to my stomach which was the part that I hated because I felt it was really ugly.

One time when I went out to eat at a seafood restaurant in Sacramento California, I was obsessed about the kind of food that I would eat to help me stay thin so I would try to avoid foods that would make me fat.

 Author: Chelby Morgan

I heard that meat was not good for good diets. What I failed to realize was that I had to eat some meat to keep some protein in my diet so that I wouldn't keep talking about how hungry I was at night.

I gave in to eating meat with the feeling that I wanted to get rid of it by throwing it all up in the bathroom but when I got in the bathroom, I didn't do that because I thought how disgusting it was for me to do it in the first place. Besides I can watch what I ate or go on a hunger strike to keep myself so-called healthy. I even didn't want to drink any milk. I was convinced that the kind of milk that was good was Soy Milk so thats what I drank.

I liked to drink Soy milk and have it in my cereals and smoothies and I won't drink any other milk beside Soy milk. Soy milk is very awesome. I think for me, the obsession to be thin went on until I was around 20.

Then I noticed that I started to slowly inculcate snacks into my diet especially when I got hungry. I enjoyed the house we lived in till I was 20 then we moved to the house my parents purchased that we live in today.

At first I thought that I was going to miss the old house because of all of the classical adventures it offered to me. The old house was very classical because it was built in 1982 and had some classical pieces that came along with it.

Well as I heard on the cartoons, out with the old in with then new so we got some stuff together for the move and moved out. Now we have been living in our new house for some 4 years. I really like it and wouldn't change it for nothing. My adult years are always off on a good start and I hope to keep it that way.

CHAPTER 6

My Social Life

My Social Life

I am excited to say that my social life is going great right now because I have really good friends that I can't complain about. I have friends that I hang out with, do stuff together with and have outings and gatherings together with.

For instance, I went to La Cabana with a group of friends in the city of Suisun, located on Main Street by the waterfront. It was hosted by a friend who wanted to do this for young people and in order to get to know us all a little bit better.

We all had a limit and we stuck to it. Everyone was happy with what they ordered. Three of my friends in the group got a super burrito with sour crème and avocado in it. It looked delicious. Now that I think about it, I should've got that because I really love burrito's, but I wasn't sure if I should get it at the time.

But now that I think about it again, the next time that I go, I will be getting myself a super burrito because their burrito looked awesome. I do recommend La Cabana because they are awesome for their nicely authentic Mexican food and appetizers.

La Cabana appetizers really get to me because when the first batch of the appetizer chips is gone, I usually can ask for another plate before my order gets to my table. The last time that I went to La Cabana, I had about two batches of chips until my order came.

Author: Chelby Morgan

The next to the last time I went by myself, I ordered a taco salad on two occasions with sour crème, whole beans, tomatoes, lettuce, meat, guacamole, and cheese inside a taco salad shell.

As much as I like taco salads, I really wanted to switch up my food choice and try something new because at La Cabana, you are never limited to a certain kind of food. Instead they have a variety such as tacos and re-fried beans.

That is something I don't always want to order. This is because I am sometimes used to eating them at home and felt why should I eat them out at a restaurant. If I go to eat at La Cabana restaurant, I prefer eating there since it is authentic.

Tacos at home just doesn't cut it for me. Places like La Cabana or even Chevys that offer semi-big portions does cut it for me. In fact, they give you so much you have to take a baggy home to eat for later especially if you don't feel like eating the rest in one sitting.

I went back to La Cabana with friends and when an order for tortillas came to our table, I opened the lid and got about three without my friends even having a chance. My friend who sat at our table next to me asked who ate them, because they thought about getting some for her mom.

She always thinks about her mom when she is at any restaurant that she eats at because her mom is like a best friend to her the same as my mom.

Anyway, after new tortillas came I sneaked a few tortillas from her stash. I put the bowl back all nice and neat before anyone noticed. That's what being in stealth mode was all about for me because when you get in stealth mode over food, you have to maintain stealth and act like it never happened.

She never bothered to ask about the stash. I guess it was because there was more to go around. Then after that, I got my order for a burrito bowl and ate away before I called it a day. I had to take a bag home and save the rest of my meal for dinner.

At home I planned to doctor it up more with my own ingredients. When dinner time came, I started to doctor up my burrito bowl with more fixings like cheese, cucumbers, tomatoes, a little bit of meat, and sour crème. Then when my doctoring of the food got done, it was time for me to eat and grub down. Then I lived happily ever the end.

My friends mom (Mrs. J) is always a good friend to me no matter how much older she is then me. When it comes to friendships with other people, I have no age barriers or limits with them. Anybody can be my friend no matter how old or young.

I will treat even older ones just like they are younger than they really are, because I heard that age is just a number. I like being her friend because she is always thoughtful, selfless, kind, nice, sweet, always laughing and has a great sense of humor, is kind and friendly.

Author: Chelby Morgan

She is also kid friendly in the sense that, when I had a friend who had a young baby at the time, she would always take the time to teach her, spend time with her, babysit her, do stuff together with her, and help her mom raise her.

When my friend's daughter was a baby, she was the cutest with fair skin, chubby legs, nice onesie, good hair, semi-fat stomach, and big cheeks. Of course, I came along into the picture and started holding her and pinching her cheeks. She at first didn't mind but then in time it came to be a problem for her so I had to stop. I like babies and if I could babysit babies then it would be no problem for me.

Now that I think about it, there was this offer to care for babies at a daycare but I turned it down and now sometimes I think that I should've taken that offer because I love babies and their cuteness. If I had the opportunity to watch babies at a daycare again then I would jump at that opportunity because babies are something that I love and care for.

Babies would be no problem for me because I really would be attached to them. Sometimes I will volunteer to hold babies because I see how cute they are and I just wouldn't mind how heavy they were as long as I was strong enough to keep them held with no difficulty.

I even thought about the possibility of being married and having a baby because if I did and it was a girl, hopefully it would look like my sister.

When she was little and was stuck in her walker with her cute clothes and a big grin on her face I would look at her and admire her cute smile all day long. I still have a picture of my sister when she was a baby and she is so cute and was always smiling with her big cheeks, bottle, pacifier, big stomach, nice pink socks, onesie, cute curly afro, and big smile on her face.

One of my favorite things about my sister when she was a baby was her face, afro and cute pouty lips. Her lips made her look chubby. If I get married and have a baby, hopefully I will have a girl that looks like my sister when she was a baby. But then again, babys grow up and having children wouldn't be fun because you will never stop being a mother. Being a mother involves caring for them and being concerned about them even when they become legal adults so that could also be a no-win situation. So for now, I like the memory of my sister as a baby.

The kind of babies I also like are chubby, cute and cuddly because the more they are those things, the better. Both of my brothers were both cute and chubby babies. Babies don't object to any sign of affection or if they are being picked up or someone smiling at them. When I thought about having a baby with my husband, I also thought will it be worth it in the long run. My conclusion led me to abandon the idea altogether and focus on my career as an aspiring author.

Author: Chelby Morgan

I have people and friends that want to support me in being an author. That feels really good to me because I've been wanting to be a author since I was younger. The thought of me being an author was something that came to mind because I felt that because I read so many books maybe I could write a book that centered around me and my life where people could read and get help from.

If two people lets say a boy and girl with my disability is inspired by my life story and how I get through with life despite my autism, then that is good for me. Speaking of dealing with autism, I have another friend that works for people who have autism. There is some who have autism so bad they can't swallow food without assistance. I told her about my book and she said it would be helpful because she is dealing with children who have autism.

I have another friend dealing with a school with children who have it. Some have autism so severe they speak in third person mode which was a new term I learned while writing my book.

For me when I hear about certain friends of mine who work with children who have autism, I feel a little bit juiced because I can help them and I can relate and tell them how I am dealing with it successfully. Also my friend is a twin and has a sister who is the same age as her. That is always useful because she loves to babysit.

When she comes over my house she knows to behave and wipe her little feet so that carpet doesn't get dirty.

I definitely understand because if it were me, I wouldn't want any dirty carpets either; instead I would like to keep them spotless at all times period.

I have really good friends that give each other's numbers and sometimes we even do stuff together such as the mall or dinner at the house. One time, on one occasion, we got together and went to the mall because we had a coupon for Bath and Body Works inside the mall. So we got in her car she drove to the mall. Once there, we hit Bath and Body Works and started stocking up on perfume, lotion and some body washes that were on sale.

I even got something for my mom so that when she got back from her trip, she would receive a present from me. My mom and my brother were in Georgia at the time and didn't get back until Saturday. When she got her present she was really happy. So that went pretty well. I like doing stuff for my mother and giving her presents as well because she mean so much to me.

I have to say that my mom is the best mother that I have ever had and she always gets in with the title of Mother of the Year as a result of all the things that she did for all of us when we were kids and how she care and love for us still does down to this day.

And if she were to win an award, she would get a Best Mother in the World medal because she fits being the recipient of that title. She is the kind of mother that some people wish they could have in their lives.

Author: Chelby Morgan

When I was born, she said it was the best thing that had ever happened to her. At my birth right then and there, I knew she wanted to have me as the smile on her face always showed. Ever since I was a baby, I was always protected because she didn't want anything to happen to my little delicate skin so she took measures to make sure that I was clean and protected from germs like any mother would.

She would wash my hair and dress me in nice clothes with fun colors like floral and purple. In one picture that I have right now, I have a face and lips that make me feel like I look like my sister when she was little.

I think of when my sister was a baby because she looked like me when she was little. We both had the same kind of lips and facial features. When I was five I had the best blessing that a kid could ever ask for. It was for a little sister. I always would jump up for joy at having a little sister because, down to this day we love each other like never before and it is all thanks to my mom who made sure I had the best sister that one could ever have.

From the moment the moment she could walk and talk, we were always playing with each other with our dolls and other toys we had. Once we had some Betty Spaghetti Dolls and we would play with them. We sometimes had our differences with each other but we stuck with each other through thick and thin.

In one apartment we had in Vallejo, we shared a room with the same bunk together and we would talk with each other and sometimes help each other get some candy at night because sometimes we both had a sweet tooth. When we got some candy, we hid them so no one would know or we would eat them right away.

I remember having things like cookies and sweets in my lunch bag for when I was finished with school. I would save some food so that when we're alone, we could eat it in our room together without my parents always knowing about us spoiling our dinner.

Sometimes when I didn't want my parents to find about all the food that I saved for me and my sister, I would rush my sister into eating it so that the evidence would be hidden from them. Sadly it didn't always work because my cover was blown and we had to stop eating in our room. Ants blew our cover.

If we didn't get caught with the stash the ants would get to it. Mind you we had been doing this for a while until we had to retire from it. When I got older and had my own room, I was very particular about how I kept my room because I did not want any part of it to be dirty. I wanted my room spotless or I would have lost it because dirty rooms are not rooms that I don't think I could ever get used to. I never will either. When I say my room was spotless it was from top to bottom without any speck of dirty in it.

Autistically Speaking

In my room, the first thing that I had was carpet and I made sure it was clean to the tee by vacuuming my floor and leaving no room for hair, dirt, clothes, shoes, paper, books, or anything else that didn't belong on the floor.

My mom or dad didn't even have to ask me to clean it up. It was automatically done because when they and my siblings and other relatives entered my room, clothes in my closet would be hung up, shoes would be organized correctly and things on my shelf were not left in any way because it had to be organized to my standards so as not to leave a speck of un-organization on any level of the shelf.

My desk was very organized and straightened out to a tee because nothing would be left all disheveled or out of place. If I needed to find important items, documents or schoolwork, it had to be in a way that I could locate it.

I don't like having to go search high and low for my stuff. I even had a TV on top of my desk and that would be dusted on a regular basis. For me to have dust accumulated on my TV set would not fly with me and reminded me of allergens and pesky dust mites that comes out to annoy humans and make them sick with more allergens.

To prevent get sick with allergens I would dust and dust and dust on a regular basis. Along with having my own bedroom, I had my own bathroom which I was told that it was a luxury because not a lot of people get have their own bathroom with their own privacy.

So I made sure to show my appreciation for it by maintaining it. I loved to keep it clean and spotless and made sure to clean sweep, mop and scrub the floors. After all it was mine.

Now when it came to my toilet I had a problem with certain people using my bathroom because I felt that it was mine and I have certain standards with how my bathroom should be kept. If more people were using my bathroom they wouldn't go by my standard of how I wanted the bathroom to be kept clean. There was just absolutely no room for a dirty bathroom> I don't want it to look like a gas station or a nasty rotten run-down bathroom that came either from other unsavory places. It was just unacceptable.

Sometimes my siblings would come in my room to watch TV with me, which I thought was nice because they were able to spend some quality time with me. However when they came into my room, they had to sit on the floor because I did not want anybody jumping on my bed or even messing it up.

When I go to sit or sleep on my bed, I don't want to end up on the floor. I like being able to have the option of sitting on my bed when I wanted to relax or chill out especially when I am watching TV, reading or writing in my diary.

Sometimes my siblings would come to use my bathroom when it was necessary. This was not often because they didn't always go by my standards of how I wanted my bathroom to kept and I said no because I wanted it to stay clean.

Author: Chelby Morgan

I have to say that I get along really well with my siblings even when we have differences. As long as we live we are going to have our differences but I always learn to put up with differences and move on.

Siblings can be like one of your best friends down the road. In the end, siblings need each other more than ever. Besides, whether you believe it or not, I think siblings should be for each other and never against each other.

As long as they work out their differences, and get along with each other, they will also be peacemakers. I feel you should apologize when you offend each other and be allies. I am really thankful that I was given siblings throughout the time that I was a child because for me my siblings really helped me to feel like I had a regular childhood that I enjoyed.

When each of my siblings were born, they were such a joy and blessing to have around as brothers and sister. I am the oldest and was alone. When they were born I now had someone else I could show my affection to, hug, hold, kiss their cheeks and even play with them. When my sister started walking and she got a little bit older, we would chase each other and play toys and games with each other.

One time, we went outside with our mom's permission and had chased each other around cars in the parking lot. We had to stop because we were told it was unsafe.

Then my second brother was one that I thought was a doll because he was so cute. Me and him would start doing stuff together. We would do things like watch older kid cartoons, chase each other, play with toys, play tag, play ball games and do typical siblings stuff.

I can say that he is now my best friend because we are just like two peas in a pod, even though we don't always agree on some things.

But hey, that doesn't stop us from being brother and sister and that should never ever be the case. All siblings should be loving and caring toward one another and not always insist on having their way. People who have it only there way could end up being the loneliest people on the planet. So I would say not to insist on always having your way in the first place.

By the way, I had a few friends who insist on having a my way or the highway attitude and I found that really annoying. I do not want to be like that I find that I avoid people like that because they are never fun to be around.

Fortunately, I don't have that kind of attitude and can say that I have some good friends down to this day not like that who still are my friends that have lasted with me for more than five years. When my youngest brother came onto the scene, it was like a having a live baby doll to play with at first.

He is truly a blessing. As he got older, we all got along with him and treated him the way we would like him to treat us. It all works out well for me because having siblings has always taught me the value of having lasting and meaningful relationships with other people that you consider to be your friends.

I have many meaningful relationships with people like the nice older lady that I always consider a friend because when I first met her, she was the kind of person that I wanted to talk to by phone as well as talking to her in person. I would approach her and ask for her number and that turned out really well because we are really good friends down to this day. It all started off with us talking to each other on the phone. There were times when I would be too busy to talk to her to the point I wouldn't have time to talk. So I would make a mental note to talk to her when I got the chance.

Sometimes she'd wonder when I was going to get back with her on the phone. I told I love to talk to her on the phone but sometimes I get really busy and she understood like she always does. We do make a point to talk and eat at In-N-Out or Wendy's.

We mostly eat at Wendy's and when that happens and we get to the window, we will have different orders and then other times we will have the same orders like a pecan salad. Unlike her, I will at times get a small fry and a green tea without a whole bunch of sugar added to it.

I still have a sweet tooth to this day. I at first thought I wasn't going to like tea. As soon as I started drinking it, I got to the point when I got halfway done, I would tell her how good it was and that I liked it very much even though I didn't think I was going to like it.

She was glad and we were both happy at that. After a while, I come to realize that certain tea can keep you going to the bathroom. So although I do recommend the green tea I say be careful because it could make you run to the bathroom once and awhile. So drink it with caution. One time, me and my friend talked about getting together for some pizza and a movie at her house. I jumped up at that thought because that's something that I like to do because I am a pizza lover. I couldn't wait even when she didn't specify a date. I'd anticipate it just in case she asks.

I tell you older ones are wonderful to have as friends despite the age difference. When I think about it, if I just hang out with only people that are my age then life would be not be that fun. In my book you should have a little fun and amazing friendship with all ages in your life. Its ok to switch it up a bit and come on out of your circle for a change.

Ever since I was little, making friends was no problem and then sometimes it was because I was the newbie at school. I would introduce myself to different people that I didn't know and talk to them like as if I had been knowing them for years. I considered myself as a social butterfly.

Author: Chelby Morgan

I sorta still am because I will always be the one to come out of my circle and introduce myself to new people and go from there. This is how you will have lifelong friends.

The kind of friends I have are real friends that look out for me and have my back at all times despite my flaws and imperfections. Friends that love you even though you may not be the prettiest or most handsome guy in the universe, they love and accept you for you. I always want to prove myself to be a good friend by showing kindness, consideration, loyalty, and selflessness.

I would say that my social life is full of purpose and meaning because I do fun stuff with my friends. We look out for each other and go on picnics, gatherings, trips and shopping sprees.

When we have parties, we will not let them get out of control to the point where police have to be called to intervene and arrest people. Also, when the party is over, everyone that can stay will help clean up to make the load light for the host.

Before I have seen other parties that other people go to, they leave it up to the host to clean up. As soon as the party is over they will leave without even lending a helping hand. To me that is a little selfish. That's the kind of people I want to learn from nor is that the crowd that I want to like.

At our parties we all will clean up when we are done having fun and sometimes we will take leftovers home when the host doesn't want left over food.

In a nutshell our parties are fun and turn out well for all parties involved. Sometimes, we will even get together for picnics and play sports and games together before getting together for a really nice Barbeque that has been freshly cooked on the grill.

Then when that is said and done, we will enjoy settling down for a sweet treat such as cake, pie, candies and ice-cream. We get down when it comes to enjoying ourselves because we will have good laughter with each other. Some of us catch up on stories from the past and converse with each other on topics like current events and other things they prefer to talk about as well.

Then when it is time for all to go home, like I said, we will pitch in and help clean up and some will take some stuff home so that no leftovers ever get wasted. As part of a real family and friends, we are not keen on wasting good food and take measures to make sure we don't throw anything away.

I will also say that my uncle is one of my best friends. There are many things that I like about him. One is he is business-oriented is not the lazy one or waste time. When he wants to accomplish something, it is done.

Once my cousin Jr was in trouble and got popped in his head for rolling his eyes at my uncle and I got popped to. I asked why and he said for good measure and that I was not exempted due to my disability so get in line.

I loved how he always treated me like the rest of the kids. I really love my uncle because he is like a second father to me and will always be my best friend. My aunt is also a gem because she is so nice as well.

I have other family and relatives that will always be my best friends for life because of they all display love to me all my life and treated me as if I don't have any disability. In fact around them I forget I have a disability. It is such a wonderful blessing to have a family like mine. I wouldn't exchange that for nothing because they will always be my heart and treasure.

They are that precious and valuable to me that I don't ever want to lose them. If I lost them to anything like death, it would totally break my heart because they are my everything.

My mom is someone I could not stand to lose because she is one that I have the most solid relationship with. I love her like no other. She is my mother and it is a blessing to have a mother who will always be in my life.

I will always be in her face asking for hugs and kisses because I know she needs and craves them. So I put forth real effort in persisting in order to make sure that she gets the love that a person like her needs. I feel a person who goes through life without affection do not function correctly.

On the other hand a person with tons of affection will also do just fine. My relationship with my mother is solid as well as with my father. I will make sure he gets enough hugs to last him for a lifetime so that he doesn't feel left out because he deserves hugs too. I love him for being the wonderful papa that he is right now and I wouldn't change that for the world. I even have a great relationship with my grandmother who lives out of state that I talk to by phone. She appreciates hearing from me and she said it makes her feel really good.

Hopefully after all this pandemic she will be able to visit California because I have been missing her for some time. I will always love her forever. I have a friend I met out of state in 06 and from that point on, I call her on the phone and send her letters to make sure she knows that I care about her.

That's what friends are for. She even once sent me a special gift which were socks, I wanted and a special gift from Bath and Body works that was also something I was most grateful for. She was really nice to do something like that for me, so I showed myself thankful and sent her a phone call and thank you letter at that. We are still friends down to this day and I would keep it that way forever. I am grateful for the social life that I have right now and wouldn't ask for more because it is neither too big or too small; it is just right.

CHAPTER 7

D.O.R.

D.O.R.

If you are autistic you have many professional supports. D.O.R. stands for Department of Rehabilitation and they specialize in helping developmentally disabled adults to find jobs and live independent and successful lives.

It also assists in job coaching for interviews and job searching. It will even help you go to school and apply for financial aid. Well because of my disability I receive social security and happen to fall on a letter that told me that I had a work ticket that qualified me for special programs that helped me look for jobs and apply for job placement.

Well when I got that work ticket, I immediately called the number for that and spoke to a representative who helped me to find the right program and that's how I found the Department of Rehabilitation in my hometown.

They are the best and very helpful. So ever since 2012, I had been going to Department of Rehabilitation to get assistance. I usually start off by speaking to a job counselor who first got my information and evaluation to see where I was at and where my job skills and everything else was concerned.

My Department of Rehabilitation first started off with helping me to get a job at different places in the store such as Walmart for once.

One time when she tried to help me apply for a position at Walmart, she wanted me to go get my dad and see what he thought about it and he didn't think that it would work for me because in retail they don't always explain things to you because they want you to get it the first time.

They just won't repeat themselves to you the second time. So therefore, we abandoned that idea and decided to focus on what I was really good at and that was by means of getting started on different evaluation tests such as shapes and other multiple choice questions were concerned. It took awhile but when it was over, I was really glad because I just wanted them to evaluate me and send me where I could really get a good job instead of a typical job at fast food or even retail.

When I first met the job counselor on the phone, I thought she would be either Asian or Hawaiian but turns out that she wasn't because she looked like a totally different in person then what I thought. She was really nice and was very helpful in my behalf and was so polite. She took down some information for me, asked me a few questions such as what my goals were for my job, and even gave me my first D.O.R.

Textbook to study, look over and even answer a few questions that were in there. I really liked her and had her for a while until she got promoted to another position in another area.

That being the case, I got a letter in the mail that informed me about the new job counselor that I would be getting and the reason why the other one left. Then the letter further gave me some information such as the new job counselor's number and email as well.

So with that information, I called her and when she didn't answer, I left her a message saying my name and personal information telling her that I called and that I am here to receive more information and assistance from her. She was a very busy woman who had her off days set for her so if you wanted to get in touch with her, you had to call her when she was available or you would either leave her a message or wait until she got back into her office.

Oh when she got important messages on her voice mail, she would eventually get back with me and go over some personal information with me and assign me a wonderful job coach who was always happy to help, flexible and willing to let me choose a place that I wanted to go to in order to discuss what job she had picked out for me as far as my job skills were concerned.

When my new job coach was assigned to me, she would schedule a time and place to meet me at and we happened to meet at a place called McDonald's which was in Suisun.

When we got there, my mom was allowed to sit in with me and help me because this was new for me. As the time progressed, my worker told me that I would be getting paid training where I would be working at the local Food Bank in town and I would work three days a week for 3-4 hours.

This seemed exciting. I had to where closed toed shoes to prevent my feet from getting hurt or dirty. So I started my first day of work at the Food Bank and begin my job of bagging up produce and tying it together in order to get it ready for distribution.

I wasn't working by myself because I had a few more people help me bag up produce and get it ready for distribution as well. I met some really nice people such as the manager of the Food Bank and the supervisor as well.

The manager was really nice because in the middle of bagging up produce, he would tell me some of his life stories before asking me what my goals were. I told him some of my goals and that reaching my goals were important. I wasn't the type to be quick to get married anytime soon and he said he totally understood and didn't pass any judgment about it.

Then there was another guy who helped with produce and he also worked the forklift that helps in assisting him to move heavy boxes up on shelves and out of doorways. He also was like an assistant to the manager as well because whatever the manager needed, he did it for him.

He also was responsible for getting some rowdy boys back into the group and out of other people's way because when one girl and another guy were helping me, they came in and as soon as they did, and it was time for one boy in my group to leave, he did not hesitate to get up and leave probably because of the fact that he didn't want to deal with them.

I could understand because I wanted to leave as well but I couldn't because I had a few more hours before I could go home and call it a day. There were a lot of very obnoxious, rowdy, ratchet and foul boys that also worked there. One boy bragged about not taking baths for days and his buddy gave him a handshake and told him that he was gangster for not doing so, but I really thought he should take a bath because he smelled bad.

Another guy was obnoxious as well because he said he was a gangster and he cursed and acted foul. When they saw us ladies they called themselves wanting to keep us company, so they went over to our table to help with bagging our produce but they kept carrying on with their loudness and obscene talk to the point where I had to get my job coach to get the manager for me, while I went out and took my walk.

Then when I came back, they were gone away from the table that I was at and I thought it was good.

Then it was time for them to go to their mentor program and some of them complained about it saying that they didn't want to go, but I didn't care because I felt that it was about time to leave and stay out of my hair for they were really annoying and just a bunch of troublemakers.

Mind you they were bunch of delinquent children who were already in trouble with the law and were forced to do community service at the Food Bank before going off to the mentor. One guy even had his nerve to ask one girl in my group for her number and she said no because he was a kid and he was in trouble.

I was glad that she didn't because he was not a gentleman and had no cooth or manners in the first place anyway. After they were gone, I was relieved and finished up my work before going home.

When it came to the last day to work at the Food Bank I was going to miss it and then again not miss it. It was something that I really enjoyed doing. It was not to difficult to have to say goodbye to the Food bank job and I now had to go look for other jobs to work at.

The Food bank was kinda an awesome place to work at and there was a few nice people there such as the manager and the supervisor of the place, and some who I bagged up produce with.

The sorting mail before dispatching it for distribution was fun as well. I liked it allowed some flexible time for a break that I had and I was able have 30 minutes for lunch and go out for a walk because it didn't take me a lot of time to eat my food because I don't take an hour to eat anything.

So when I got done with my food, I went outside to go for a walk until my break was over. Then I went back to work until it was time to go home for good. When I worked, I always felt the rewards of working hard when I would have In-N-Out burgers one time and had a well-deserved meal such as a hamburger and some vegetables and potatoes to go with it as well.

The food bank job lasted for two weeks and when that was over I said goodbye and focused on looking for other jobs elsewhere. Me and my couch met at our usual spot to discuss job goals and help me apply for jobs that I was good at. There was one job that she helped me to apply for and that was Pride Industries which specializes in helping disabled adults to get jobs within the industry itself. I applied for that job and sent in my resume and every little document that was needed in getting the job.

After a week of applying for the job, I would call to follow up and they would tell me to call back and when I did they would either be out of their office or on vacation. I kept at it until they called me back and said the position was already filled.

Author: Chelby Morgan

When I heard the news, I was really disappointed because I wanted to work and I didn't care what the position was as long as I was working. The disappointment lasted for a few minutes until I had to move on and find another job.

The job that I stumbled on was the job for a Pre-K position at a community center right by the library. My job coach and I crossed the street to get to that place and we were on time for the interview even though we had to wait for a few minutes because they were interviewing other candidates for the position as well.

When they were done interviewing them, they called my name and interviewed me as well. They liked my answers and considered hiring me but they called me back to say that the position had already been filled so I had to keep looking for another job until I finally could get a job.

As part of the D.O.R. Program, they specialize in providing monies for interview clothes such as dress pants, skirts, shirts and shoes because one time in the process of preparing me for a possible interview or two, we went to Ross to shop for those clothes and I tell you that I have had clothes for a year or so.

I had three interviews so far so I would wear those clothes to look professional. I really liked her because she was so wonderful and awesome and when I couldn't make it she would make another appointment for me to make the next following week.

After a while though, she accepted another position at a special place where they also have programs to help people get jobs and schooling as well and it wasn't for just disabled adults. It was for everybody. So when she left I had another job coach that helped me to find a job until I landed a position as crew at McDonald's.

I would at first spend three hours looking for jobs every day until I found out that I could just look for jobs every day for only a few minutes. I kept looking for a jobs and one time I wanted to quit the whole program because I felt that I wasn't getting anywhere in finding jobs and I felt that if I could start my own business and look for jobs on my own, then that would be better for me.

I went to a job fair and had sessions where I would practice for interviews and they would have snacks, juices, and coffee for the participants. They would have stations set up such as Six Flags, Nelson Staffing and Pride Industries the same one I tried to apply for earlier.

I choose those three jobs and they interviewed me and I couldn't take all of them so I had to keep searching until I could finally get a job at McDonald's because I was close to quitting the program because I felt that I was going nowhere. I did get a job at McDonald's and I worked there for a while, but I quit because of so much drama going on there. I did leave on good terms and that's all that mattered the manager told me.

I got my resume together with the help of a job coach and I can live independently. Overall, all the Job Coaches and personal assigned to me from Department of Rehabilitation were most definitely some of the best and kind people I ever met. Some were busier than others, but they all were really good.

I would recommend Department of Rehabilitation program to anyone who has a disability so that they too can get help to live independent, successful, and live happy lives. Department of Rehabilitation provides wonderful programs for schooling, job placement, job search, interview clothes and shoes, job fairs, and a job coach and a location to meet at for job appointments that is convenient for the client and job coach.

They also provide paid training to get you started with some experience and they help you to get resumes together so that it can look professional and might open the doors for a potential job. When you go for that program you will never regret it and I can say that from experience.

CHAPTER 8

My Daily Routine

Author: Chelby Morgan

My Daily Routine

As life continues to go on, I think it is a must for me to have a schedule and routine in order to have organization in my life. If you do not like to have a schedule you are in for disaster and disappointment. Schedules and routines are a must to have in life if you are to be successful and stress free.

To start off, I have a daily routine of cleaning my room once a week so that my room can stay tidy, clean, and neat. I will start by changing my sheets and pillowcases once a week to avoid bed bugs and maintain a level of sanitation and standard cleanliness.

Sometimes I will even wash my pillowcase liner to ensure cleanliness. That helps keep bed bugs from inhabiting my pillowcase and my skin for that matter. I even spray Lysol around my bed and my pillow so that it can deodorize.

For the bed frames on my bed, I will get a dusting cloth and dust them to minimize the increase of dust that is sitting on top of the frame so that it doesn't cause allergies or dander to increase and multiply because those things are no joke.

When it comes to cleaning my window and window seal, they will not get passed up because I don't like for my windows to be dirty so I start cleaning the window by using fabuloso to clean the window and a vacuum to vacuum all dirt and dirty particles off the window seal. Sometimes I will even wipe it off myself.

For the door that leads to my bedroom, I will dust and clean the door seals off to make sure that it stays clean because to me, a door never looks good when it is filled with dirtiness and filth on it. It just doesn't sit well with me so it has to get cleaned on a regular basis once a week.

Even the desk in my room gets cleaned by means of dusting the bottom, top, and middle and inside of the desk to insure not even a speck of dust gets close to it. Then when I am done with that job, I will go through my stuff to organize it the way that I want it to be organized.

I will start off by organizing papers and notebooks in a certain way that I want it to be done so when I am done organizing, it will be stacked neatly and in their place. This includes my smallest notebooks on top of the largest notebooks.

In that way nothing is disheveled or out of order. I have some things on top of my desk such as figurines, lotion, a lamp, storage cases and box full of tissues that never go ignored when it comes to neatness and organization. When I must dust the top of my desk, I move things off my desk and onto my bed so that I can dust the desk fully for a real clean.

When I am done with that, I will put everything back where in a certain way that I want them to be organized. I may set things from largest to smallest before putting the lotion neatly in front of it.

Author: Chelby Morgan

Then sometimes when I have to put back storage cases in their rightful places, I will set them at the edge of my desk to my left side with the biggest storage cases going on the bottom and the medium-smallest storage case going on the top so in that way it's not too much for me to locate stuff that I needed for the day and even weeks to come.

Then I have stuff at the bottom of my desk. If my family members look at my stuff, I do not want them to conclude that I hoard stuff or have a dirty desk because I try to organize everything to the tee. When I am done dusting the bottom of the desk, I have a certain way of organizing I even put my computer laptop next to a bag full of drawings, drawing pads, pencils and pens, colored pencils, crayons, folders, and extra book writing documents. With that being said, I will put a bag full of clothes that need some altering on top of that bag until I can go inside the alteration store to get it fixed.

I then will put my book bag next to it. Finally, my purse will go next to it and with all those things next to each other, they will be as neat and tidy as I can get it. For my clothes that go in my closet, whenever I get clothes all washed and dried, they will first be folded up and put in my storage drawer that I use when I am done. If you want to know where I purchased the bins it was at Wal-Mart for a good deal.

I had thought of getting a storage container for all my clothes when I was shopping at Wal-mart. My shelving unit was once down the tubes because I needed a little bit more organization than what I was getting with almost everything out and a mini beige storage container that I had been keeping on top of my shelf for the longest in order to keep my socks, underwear, bras, and scarves in place.

I had been doing that for a while until my shelving unit went down the tubes. I came up with the idea to get my own storage unit for my clothes when my sister would get some storage unit for her clothes. I thought I would need a little bit more organization than what I was getting before those things came about.

So now that I have my own storage I have a little bit more room in my closet for all of my clothes, jewelry, toiletries and towels for my body and face. In my closet, when I put up my clothes, they will be rolled up or folded in a certain way to ensure that they are as neat and tidy as they can be.

So that being the case, when I need to get clothes to wear or a sock or anything to make myself look nice or feel comfortable, I can locate my stuff easily and not stress over what I am going to wear. First off with the top of my storage drawer goes my tank tops and a little bit of my summer clothes when the summertime comes.

When winter comes, scarves, hats and tank tops will go into the drawer and they will always be folded up and put in a way that will be neat and easy to find especially when I need and want something from the top drawer to wear when I am either going out or just want to take it easy and relax. For the second drawer goes my socks, and undergarments.

I never worry about folding them up because to me they are small and just undergarments so why bother folding them up in the first place. Besides you'll always be able to find them and match them up with whatever you want to match them up with and still look cute and fashionable.

Now for third and last drawer goes my pants ha-ha that was so easy because when I need pants, capri or even shorts to wear, I can find those in a hot minute and still look all hot and fashionable. My fashion can rock California or anywhere in any town anywhere on the globe of the earth.

Then on top of my storage cases goes my two pink storage cases with extra clothes to fit in those bins and in one bin will go my pants and some shirts and cardigans. The other bin will have some dress shirts, one dress, and a few shirts and workout shirts to top off because when I fold up my workout shirts I will stack up all my workout shirts on top of each other and fold them altogether like you would with a taco and then call it a day.

My dress shirts, dress and skirts never have to worry about being folded up because they automatically get hung up so that makes the laundry and folding up clothes job a lot easier for me.

I have certain skirts that need to be ironed on a hanger before getting out the ironing board. I iron all skirts at once so that I don't have to do them at the last minute. Afterwards I will hang them back up in a neat way so that they don't have to be ironed again and can quickly get them out of my closet and put on with no hassle. My corduroy jackets will be hung up on a handle in the middle of my closet right where my body towel is located.

I find that if I move them over, I will find more stuff behind them which consists of a jewelry box full of jewelry, a storage box for panty liners, a box for nail polish, money container with a box of qtips next to it, and a little brown box that contain photos, thank you cards and allot of my good ole memories.

I try and organize in a way that won't bust my shelving unit and will stay neat and tidy. For my top shelf even though I share that with my sister, I will have the right side to myself and she will have the left to herself.

So that being the case, even my right shelf is organized in such a way even though my sister and I share a caddy for our ponytail holders and hair products. It still is kept on the shelf and in its place as well.

In the caddy, the ponytail holders will go in one little small section of the caddy while the other will go into another section of the caddy and my sister's head bands, oil and edge control will go into the biggest section of the caddy.

Beside my caddy goes my personal my yarn kit and beige storage container that has been folded down ever since I got my storage container. Even during COVID-19, my friends on social media can see my room and how organized I keep it.

They say that they would feel comfortable coming into my room. Under no circumstances will I allow anyone to sit on my bed. I don't want anyone to mess up my bed or sheets so to keep that from happening, no one is allowed on my bed except me.

Every six months my sister and I would switch from being on top or bottom bunks. Regardless of which, I managed to keep my bed neat and clean and never put too much pressure on it. All the neat, clean and organizing habits that I have for my room reminds me of what I used to be at my previous houses.

When my family moved into a nicer house, I would create certain ways that I wanted to keep my room. In case I have guests I want everything neat when it comes to my room.

Even though my parents set rules on how each family member should keep our rooms and bathroom, I would take it to the next level by cleaning and organizing the bathroom and my bedroom to the tee. No one ever needs to remind, ask, or bribe me to do it.

Autistically Speaking

It is automatic for me to keep things clean and tidy. I also kept my closet neat and organized. Although I did not have much in there, I still made sure everything in it was hung up and put into a rightful place. I feel a sloppy closet with clothes that are on the floor or not hung up was unacceptable.

One reason why I have my own room was because my parents knew me to be the clean and tidy one who never leaves anything on the floor or out of place. As I got older, I found that I needed my own space that I could call my own.

Even though my siblings and I share a bathroom, I made sure to keep it clean even if I did not mess it up. I knew any one of us would clean the bathroom. I get frustrated if the bathroom is not clean because I like to see a bathroom clean. I see commercials on tv that shows bugs and roaches found in bathrooms and fortunately that has never been the case.

I also researched online and if you don't want bugs in your house or ants, then you should take special measures to keep them out. One of the measures that I took was not eating in my room nor leaving any candy wrappers on the floor because that is one thing that attracts bugs to your bedroom.

I remember when I had candy in my backpack, ants used to be found crawling inside and my mom told me it was a result of leaving popcorn seeds, candy, and fruits in my backpack.

Author: Chelby Morgan

I thought I could close it but even then if I left those things inside it, the ants would find a way into my backpack and start munching on whatever was left inside it.

With that being the case, I made sure I didn't have any food left in my back packs especially if I did not want to deal with ants. I personally do not want to have anything to do with ants because they make me itch just looking at them.

I also never brought wanted to bring any food in my room to avoid ants coming. I did only on a few occasions if I was sick. Getting sick was very seldom. I do remember on occasion if I had a cold or fever, my mom or dad would have food brought to my room. It usually was soup and crackers or anything to munch on. What was brought to me was fine with me because whenever I was sick, I did not want anything extra that required crumbs or cleaning.

I remember when I had my own bathroom, everybody wanted to either use it or just look at it because my bathroom was spotless. You could not find even a speck of dust in it. What's kinda funny was when I went to school. This one guy who I had a crush on tried to make fun of me about keeping my room so clean.

I would tell him that if he does not like to a clean room then he can live in a pig sty. I would always find ways to get in a last word hoping he would not make fun of me.

Sometimes I would say things about his pigsty just to annoy him before he had the chance to say anything to me. Things would heat up between us. He would talk about my neatness and I would talk about his pigsty. By the end of the conversation it would cool down between the both of us and we would get along with each other in the end.

At this time, we lived in Georgia and was set to California where I then would have to share a room with my sister.

At first, I didn't want to share a room but I quickly got used to sharing a room with my sister. For me it got to the point where I always wanted her company, and I would attach myself to her. Even though we shared a room together, I still had standards of how I wanted our room to be kept clean and I expected her to follow them.

Needless to say it didn't always work out well because she had her own ideas. For instance, we shared a desk together and I wanted the desk to be a certain way. She then would move stuff around and I would take it upon myself to clear it off. She then would get up and tell my mom on me.

My OCD in cleaning did at times drive her crazy she told me but she managed to deal with me and got over it because we still had to share a room and with each other. Whenever my cousins Erika and Nell would come over I had standards for them as well to follow in my room.

I told them I wanted my bed to be kept clean and did not want them to sit on it whatsoever. Nell would say there is nothing special about my bed and that my bed was only a spring mattress. I disagreed with her and would tell her it was not a spring mattress because I used it all year round.

One time when they came over and Nell sat on my bed, I told her to get off because I didn't want her on it. I felt that she would jump on my bed and break it and I did not have time for that to happen. I wasn't about to get it broken to the point where I had to sleep on the floor so I told Nell to get off my bed, but she wouldn't listen. She said she just wanted somewhere to sit and had a dress on.

So I agreed to let her sit on my bed. I then asked her mom that if she act disorderly on my bed could she take care of it. She said she would so I then did not mind if my cousins sat on my bed.

Sometimes I think that if my sister wasn't my roommate and I had someone else as a roommate they would not last long because of my cleaning habits. My sister said I got to the point where my cleaning habits would erk her and she couldn't deal with it much longer. She loved me and stuck it out with me. That's the reason to this day we still are thick as thieves as they say.

My sister developed good cleaning habits and keeping things neat no longer bothered her. We even got to the point where we would take turns dusting, making beds, organizing our stuff, cleaning the windows, folding clothes, and organizing our storage bins.

I give my sister her props because she is a neat and wonderful sister to have. Now lets talk about the kitchen where I would clean up the counters, microwave, stove, toaster, coffee maker and sometimes the wooden cutting board.

I don't like to use the cutting board because it is just too much work in cleaning it. For some reason, my OCD about using the wooden cutting board causes me anxiety. When a wooden cutting board is being used, it creates microscopic messes deep inside the wood that one cannot see. So how could you ever thoroughly clean it? For me to clean it, I would need a magnifying glass to get deep in the pores of the wood.

A wood cutting board just doesn't sit well for me. I feel that if you use it too often then you are going to destroy the wood. So for me, I say, not to use a wooden cutting board or just give it away. The wooden cutting board is a no-no for usage in my book.

My advice would be for you to try using a glass cutting board because messes are easy to clean up and you don't have to worry about destroying the wood. Glass cutting board is recommended because messes are easy to clean and dry at the same time. With a wooden cutting board, you run the risk of cross contamination and residue being left behind in the wood. I think that the job of cleaning counters and stoves is easy because you can use this stuff called fabuloso to clean with for a nice easy clean result.

The reason why I recommend fabuloso is because it is reasonable in price, has a nice quality to it, and gives a nice spick and span easy-to-clean results. You can also use it with a napkin, paper towel or even a dish towel to wipe things with it. Also if you are concerned about residue or anything left behind, you won't ever have to worry as long as you use it right and wipe it down with a damp cloth.

Again, if you want good cleaning results, I highly recommend Fabuloso. If you want to know where to find it, look for it at Wal-mart or even the 99 cents store in any town that you reside in. I recommend that you go to the 99 cent store to purchase it because it is reasonable in price and you can even get a nice sized bottle that can last for weeks or a month.

Cleaning floors are not exempt from being kept clean the good ole fashioned way. I will get a cleaning product called Bona that is good for mopping after I'm done sweeping. Then when the mopping job is done, I will let it sit for a few minutes to let it dry before calling it a night and putting everything back in its rightful places.

Then when that's said and done, I will be free to go about my business and have some downtime for myself. In the long run, I feel really good to have a clean area to come into especially the kitchen. A clean kitchen is really something warm and inviting to go into.

With that being said, cleanliness rules and dirt is out of the door. I don't like messes or anything that's dirty.

Now about my scheduling, I like to have schedules and routine in my life because without those things, my life would just be stressful and chaotic. Every week, I will write down every little detail of the things that I will be doing from Monday to Friday.

Whenever I have things to do on the weekends or even on a Friday, I'll write them down on a piece of paper and commit to that schedule. Every morning starts off with me getting up at a time that I set for myself with a morning routine. Breakfast at a certain time which is no later than 10 in the morning before committing to doing my chores or my cleaning routines.

After my breakfast chores, cleaning are all done for the morning, I will workout. After my workout I will do some reading or studying before it's time to have lunch at a certain time in the afternoon. Lunch is usually between 12-3 in the afternoon. Four is the time to have a snack and when I work on writing this book I am currently doing right now.

I like to write my book usually on days such as Thursday, Saturday and sometimes even Wednesday or Sundays. The Sundays and Wednesdays is usually the case for me right now because I have a deadline to reach.

Autistically Speaking

I want my book sent out in June so that it can be edited and published. I want my book published for all to read. Sometimes when I write and type I will give myself deadlines to get things done. I like to keep my commitments and push myself to stay on point. My book writing career is fun, and I like putting all my thoughts on paper.

I love to schedule a whole bunch of things in advance. I do this so when something comes up or I call myself wanting to do something fun or important, I will schedule it as far in advance as possible.

Scheduling things in advance is what works for me. In that way, I think it is better organized and less stressful for me. I try and do every little and big thing in advance if possible. I don't have time to be stressed out when something important comes up and I couldn't get it because of my scheduling. I also like to do things early or on time.

Some people could live with the kind of person I am but if they don't like it, I think they are truly missing out on a nice personality and it is their loss. There you have it. You have gotten to know some of my daily aspects and routines. Hopefully it won't discourage you from getting to know people with my condition. Although I may do things a bit differently from others, I've been told by many people, they do not mind me at all and loved to get to know me and that I am a nice person.

CHAPTER 9

My Entertainment

Author: Chelby Morgan

My Entertainment

After graduating from high school with a 4.0 average and a diploma, one of the things that I got out of high school education was the fact that I liked learning about different subjects such as history, English and Psychology.

I had psychology during my senior year and even though I didn't want to have a job in psychology, I really enjoyed learning it and doing homework on it. I like it so much that I would make sure to take my time on that subject to get a good grade. With autism I had to learn to keep growing and progressing. It's wasn't easy, but it is possible.

As I look back over the years, Psychology was a good subject for me because I really got to study about different kinds of minds that other people possess, and it helped me with my disorder. Psychology also helped me in the real world especially whenever I encountered people with my disorder.

I can tell if someone has my disorder. I sometimes can tell when people have certain disorders. I think psychology helped me a little in that regards. Sometimes I know when to keep up my guard or if I need to just cut ties and contact with certain people.

I can't always tell what kind of mental disorders that other people have but when I see them act or talk strangely, it seems something is wrong. Being disabled myself, I can relate to anyone with a disorder and do not judge them.

They too are somebody's child and they didn't ask to be in the predicament that they may be in right now. I learned that disorders also can be caused by being in certain predicaments that stems from things people had to face such as abuse, or from being in a traumatizing environment.

Take for example people in different countries that are war torn, they deal with, death of a loved one constantly, economic downturns, and other sad factors that causes them disorders.

Psychology has truly paid off for me because it has made me a little bit more educated about how people's minds work in different ways. Another thing that I got out of being educated in high school was studying civics and government. I really enjoyed those classes and it helped me to see how the government works right now and what laws and regulations are in store for U.S. Citizens.

I notice that with autism in USA, you do have some resources and have others helping you. Anyone with autism should accept the help but still work hard. I did and it worked. It wasn't easy. I never feel sorry for myself even when I might really want to.

From TV, I learned about how immigration works for immigrants who desire to enter the states for better opportunities and how they get naturalized as citizens themselves.

For example, when a person comes from a different country and they get naturalized into a US citizen, they have to learn to speak English, pledge their Allegiance to the flag, get a job, and obey all the laws of this land. I've also learned about how immigrants obtain green cards. If I remember correctly, they can't run for certain office but they can stay in the country for as long as their green card allows them to stay. For some it's really hard to get into the U.S. and become a US citizen because the countries they come from may be complicated. Many times they are forced to immigrate illegally.

That can be illustrated in one book I read about two families who immigrated from Mexico to live in the U.S. One family stayed in the country illegally and the other got in the country with a green card. One family who got into the country illegally without a green card or any proof of citizenship stayed in the country but they had to be really careful not to get caught or they could be deported back to their country.

Getting deported by the way seems to be the worst because now they have to start from square 1 and deal with things much worse after being deported. I saw on TV this one guy was interviewed and he said he would hustle around and lied about his personal information when it came time to signing documents so he wouldn't be discovered, caught or arrested and deported.

The guy said he had been doing that for years until immigration laws got tougher. Another situation I saw on TV was about one girl of a family of 4 who crossed into the country illegally. She wanted to go to college and get a good career instead of working at a fast-food restaurant like her parents were doing. Because of their status, her mom could only get work at a fast-food restaurant while her dad could get work as a janitor. These jobs were easier to get for them and had more relaxed proof of citizenship.

They really had to be careful about everything in order to avoid being caught and arrested. The story about that had a good ending though because the girl grew up and graduated. She soon secured a profession as a lawyer.

She later had a child and her dad always called her a superwoman because when she was in school, she was exceptionally good at balancing her homework, school with chores and social life. By the time she became a lawyer and had a child, she already developed habits that benefited her. That was a eye opener to watch because what I have seen immigrants having to go through in order to get into this country as U.S. Citizen is sad. They do this all to try and get better opportunities for themselves and their children. It just goes to show that when you want something badly enough you can work hard and stay focused.

I also watched a documentary on PBS about this one family who entered the country illegally while one of the kids got in as a legal citizen. The mother in the documentary was a hard worker who made sure her kids were well-fed, got a good education, had clean clothing, and did fun things like parties and rodeos together. Oh and speaking of rodeos, the oldest sibling got a job as a horse rider in rodeos and he made a good lump sum of money when he won. Even when he didn't win, his mother still loved him as a son.

I wish that all parents had the same attitude because winning is not everything. Sometimes, when I go to my cousins' house, I stumble on a television show called Toddlers and Tiaras and it centered on children mostly girls that were in pageant beauty contest and they were expected to win because to the parents winning was everything for it meant money and being famous on TV. When the girls didn't win they would either cry or have a fit or worse yet feel like they were ugly or no better than the girl that won.

I really felt bad for any of the losers on the program because to me it's like they are too young to understand the concept of true beauty and what it means to be beautiful on the inside. They don't fully understand that the life style has consequences that the parents feed into them.

It also seems they sometimes spoil them with makeup, jewelry and give them anything they want to win. What is even worse is they expect them to win and any opponent who gets in the way of them winning will supposedly get their butts kicked.

I can't stand that show because I feel that the children are being exploited and expected to win when they should be outside in the yard, at school and doing stuff that involves enjoying a real childhood.

I remember when I used to think pageants were cute, but the older I got, the less desire that I had to be in them. It got to a point where I didn't think it would be cute for me to be in them. I also didn't know if I could win because you need the attitude that makes you think more of yourself than necessary.

Also if I did not win I would question the concept of what true beauty is. It then would be hard to accept my so-called flaws for what they are. So I will continue to believe what I do know that a pageant can't ever tell me and that is I am beautiful on the inside.

Besides in the long run, all the makeup and beauty products will have to come off. I wonder, what happens to life long beauty contestants? What if they attracted a husband who only saw them all glammed up? What would he say if he ever saw his beauty queen without makeup and saw all the flaws?

So I think it's best to start loving yourself at a young age without with or without all the makeup or excessive beauty products that people overly use to make themselves look beautiful. Make is not bad and I wear a little. If you do like to wear makeup, I think it should be modest and sensible instead of putting excess amounts of it on. I'm really glad that I didn't get into wearing a lot of makeup because I love myself for who I am and beauty products can't change that.

There is some entertainment that involves education which I love to watch because it fascinates me. One of the things that I watched recently was the Blue Planet. Learning about the ocean was truly fascinating because it made me feel like I was in the water myself with all the fish and the ocean that surrounded it.

There was one thing that made me feel like I would never get in certain water. Sharks! Sharks are one of the most dangerous species a human can encounter in the water. Sharks not only eat fish they bite humans hard. I saw the movie Jaws and if you ask Jaws, he would say the more meat humans have the better.

I heard waters where sharks loves to live is in Florida or Hawaii. If you go in those water at beaches in those states, and you see a sign that says shark, it can prove to be very dangerous if you.

Do not and I repeat do not go near the water at any beach that has a sign that says warning shark, or it can be over.

You really would be taking a chance at being eaten. Even if you don't get eaten, you might come out with missing limbs that will make you disabled.

My thing is, I will get in the water but not if I see a warning sign. Even then I will be extremely careful to not go very far in the water because sometimes warning signs are posted after there is a shark attack.

I'm not trying to get bit or eaten by a shark because those predators are no joke at all. For the most part, if I see a sign that says shark warning, as this famous creator of a dance TV show called soul train hosted by Don Cornelius, would say "you can bet your bottom dolla" that you won't hear me holla because I won't be getting in any water that has a shark warning sign.

That being said while I was watching the Blue Planet, I also learned that there is another kind of fish that proves to be a predator kinda like the sharks. I forgot the name of that fish but what I do know about that fish is they may be predators but for another reason.

They come so that the little fish can give them a cleaning service. When I learned about that, I thought that they must be breathing a sigh of relief because they would rather be doing a cleaning service for other kinds of fish than to get eaten by a shark.

If I were those little fish, I would be relieved to do a cleaning service for them because the last thing I wanted was to be eaten by a shark.

Author: Chelby Morgan

Autistically Speaking

Sharks are known to be very brutal and ruthless. They show now mercy nor do they play fair at all. Once they see meat, they don't care if it is a fish or human; as long as it is floating in the ocean and it looks like good meat to eat, they will go for it, attack it and make a meal out of it.

Learning and watching sharks on an educational video makes me think of some human type sharks in the real world. Human sharks see someone that is fresh clean and naive, and they will go for them and mess them up real quick. These human sharks do not care about the people that they prey on or hurt. They take advantage of their prey and eat them alive by ruining their lives.

That's why I have learned to be extremely careful about my safety and what kind of people that I decide to associate myself with. I don't want to find out at the last minute that I was taken advantage of and eaten alive by a human shark.

I think back to when I was in school and didn't realize that dating could be fatal. Young boys seemed to only be interested in their own gratification, being naïve and disabled I didn't completely understand that.

All I wanted was affection from the guys. At the time I didn't understand that it comes with a huge price. Boy am I glad I had loving parents and friends who cared about me and jumped into action the moment they saw things going south.

I dodged a bullet my dad says but could have been a victim of human sharks. That being said, I will not be some prey that human sharks decide to pick up on. I am a real human being that deserves some dignity and respect at that.

Also I learned you don't even have to be a hottie. A human shark will go to anyone that they see as easy prey. That's exactly what sharks do. I stand my ground and let those predators know to stay far away from me. I change my attitude, demeanor to not attract them. I even watch my dress and grooming.

Yeah I may be young but I'm not some fresh meat or play thing for human sharks that want to try and pick me up and leave me off on the side.

Best believe that I'm on guard watching out and will not allow predators or any perverts to come anywhere near me. In a nutshell, I am not one to be messed with. I got that saying from my uncle who people did not mess with.

And speaking of predators I saw a movie with some friends from 1979 called When a Stranger Calls.

I would have enjoyed it even more if everyone watching would have stop getting loud and talking throughout the whole movie. "Oh my goodness," while I was trying to watch the movie people on the left side of me and even behind me talking throughout the movie and just being ratchet. They were being loud and narrating the whole movie until it ended.

Author: Chelby Morgan

I don't even know if I liked the movie now that I think about it. I don't like watching movies with some people because they get loud and talk throughout the movie. This is why I prefer watching movies at home.

I like watching movies with my mom and a few select amount of people who won't talk throughout the movie or get loud to begin with. Mostly I watch movies by myself and when I do, I get more out of them and enjoy them more. I went to the library and checked out the movie When a Stranger Calls by myself.

It was different then the one I saw previously. It was like a learning tool for me because what I got out of it was that there was a teenager girl in Colorado who was going through a crisis in her life where her boyfriend was cheating on her and she went over her minutes on her phone which costed them $800.00. To pay off that debt, she was grounded for a month and had to babysit for a wealthy family named the Mandrakes.

When she got there, they gave her the tour of the house and some phone numbers for themselves and the restaurant that they were going to. I think that was smart because you may never know if you have to call the boss that you're babysitting your kids for in case of an emergency.

Well she did call the restaurant because she needed to talk to them because she felt lonely. Some creepy stalker kept calling her and then hanging up.

The downside of her having that babysitting job was that she did not think to lock the door which was very dangerous because he got into the house and almost killed her and the kids that she was babysitting.

The kids were sleeping and she was alone with no company in the house because all her friends and classmates except her went to a bonfire. That being said she was very lonely until her friend showed up before having to leave. While she was leaving and trying to start up her car, an unknown figure came up and killed her.

The girl inside tried to call her friend but there was no answer so she figured that something was up and she locked the front door, closed the curtains, and turned on the alarm and when I watched that part, I thought that she should have thought to do that when she first got into the house before she went to sit down and do her homework.

It was pretty careless to not think about doing those things because she could've gotten raped and murdered and those kids would've been next as well. She and the kids got out of the house safely but she had to be in a hospital to help get her better. While she was there, she started having nightmares and panic attacks about the whole event that had just happened.

It was so bad that the staff and her dad did their best to try to restrain her with the movie ending and the screen turning black.

Author: Chelby Morgan

That movie was ok, but there were a few things that I got out of it. One is to never go over your minutes on your cell phone that your parents happen to be paying for and if you ever get a chance to babysit somebody else's kid(s), be especially careful to lock up the doors and set the alarm if the house has one. The last thing that you want is for somebody to break into your house to do harm to you.

There was a time where if someone broke into your house, they would keep you alive and tell you not to tell anyone unless you wanted them to come back and kill you. Nowadays if someone were to break into your house, they would violate you and then kill you.

So the lesson that should be learned here is when you are either home by yourself or you're watching somebody else's kids, make sure to lock the door and keep it locked with the alarm turned on. This way if the alarm does go off, the person breaking into your house will think twice about it.

Also whenever it is night time, you can have fun either by yourself or with the kids that you're babysitting, as long as you make sure everything is locked up. Also shut the curtains as well because you don't want to give any perverts, looky-e-loos, or burglars ideas on how they can possibly break into your house.

Then when you lock up everything, make sure they are securely locked all the way so that no criminal has a way of getting into your house. Also make sure you have minutes on your cell phone to call 911 in case of an emergency.

When it comes to the front door or someone that you're not expecting to come knock, without even text, phone call or invitation and they start knocking, DO NOT never open it up for them because, if you do that, you are truly getting yourself in trouble.

You don't always know who they are and what kind of person they are on the inside. They could be scam artists or even serial killers and you would not know until it was too late. You would not get a good reference if the parents of the kids that you we're supposed to be watching come home to find either you or your kids lying on the floor dead. You could be fired on the spot. For me, when I am home by myself or I am watching my siblings, I do not need to be reminded not to open the door for anybody unless I was expecting them.

That reminds me of a movie that I saw in 2014 called <u>No Good Deed</u> and the movie was great yet a little bit scary. It centered on a woman who got killed for not being faithful to the man that did that to her. He was very upset that she wasn't being faithful to him so he took that matter into his own hands and killed her.

He would come into her house while she was making tea and call her honey. He would grill her about what man she was with and show proof of all the letters that she was writing to other men. Then while they were in another room together, that's when he killed her and left her body there to go to Tennessee and supposedly find a place to stay.

Author: Chelby Morgan

He found a woman alone with her children at the house to get some help with his wounds and stay for a while until the weather let up. Then after awhile though, his true motives started to show and he went terrorizing the family until she put a stop to it and her husband showed up to help. He ended up getting punched in the face for his infidelity only to get a divorce.

That's when she moved to Atlanta to start fresh and live an independent life as a law person. The movie had a good ending. I like movies with good endings because without them being good, then what's the point of making movies and stories in the first place.

I really got something out of the movie and is never ever open the door for anybody nor let them in the house unless you really know them as a true friend. I am even careful about who I let into my house because not only do I live with my family but I don't want to put my life or the life of my family member in jeopardy by letting in people that I don't eve know inside.

I once made a really bad mistake of that when I lived at my other house when I was home with my brother at the time. One guy was knocking at the door and I opened it because he claimed to be a PG&E guy. He had no ID to prove it so I talked but he said he was going to be back while I shut the door.

I told my parents and they asked me why I didn't have him get out his ID for me to see and why I just opened the door for anybody like him.

Autistically Speaking

They asked me what if he came in and stole stuff out of the house or hurt me and my brother. After I thought about that whole incident, I told myself that I would never do that again because that was dangerous.

When someone starts knocking at the door, my parents tell me that I am not obligated to answer the door or even respond to them in anyway. If I do see or hear them knocking at the door, I just don't answer unless I either truly know them or I am expecting them.

My Dad will answer all the knocks at the door because he is tough and can has a way to gauge what kind of person who knocks on our door. He will quickly decide if he wants to invite them in or not.

Now, if someone claims to be on fire or that my house is on fire, I still won't open up the door for them because if I do that, they might be the one to start the fire. With that in mind, if you actually see someone on fire, just call 911 who would readily come to give assistance if it is needed.

That is what I would do instead of letting them in my house. I also would not let them in because if I don't see any sign that my house is on fire to begin with then why I should let them in. It could be a scam. I'm getting better at just answering the door only for those that I'm expecting. I do not open the door for just anybody because when somebody knocks and my parents are at home, I will get my parents to answer the door.

Author: *Chelby Morgan*

Unless it is someone, I am expecting that's the only time I will open up the door for them. I am also leery about opening up doors for people especially at night and when I don't even know them because I never think that nighttime is a good time to be opening up your doors.

It's very scary with the thought of someone just walking in and maybe even harming you. Yeah I may have graduated from high school with a diploma and 4.0 GPA average in all my classes, but I never stop learning as long as I am living.

One of the few things that I have learned so far is that in certain neighborhoods, you have to be extremely careful. Some parents with young children or babies have had their babies snatched from open windows without the parent even knowing about it.

My friend brought it to my attention and when she did, I thought it was scary for her because I was thinking about her youngest daughter who has her own room but doesn't sleep in it yet.

I wonder is she scared that her child could get snatched from her window at night? It is a scary thought that a kidnapper is going take your child and by the time you wake up from your 7-8 hour of beauty rest and wake up only to find the kids missing.

Then they would start to freak out and look frantically everywhere for that child before rushing to the phone to call 911, put up missing signs and do a search party until you find that child.

The older I get the more I see missing signs of children posted up in stores and in newspaper ads than what I saw in my younger years. More and more children are getting kidnapped and taken away to different places. When there are missing signs everywhere and the parents are frantically looking for them.

With that being the case, they will even start to look for the person that kidnapped their child until that person is found and punished and just won't rest until that happens. They start to feel the person who did that to their child should be fully punished.

I feel the same way. With that information in mind, I can see why my friend is concerned for her little child's safety because like her, no parents ever wants to lose their child or children to monsters that are out to prey on innocent.

I wanted to get married and have kids one day but with all the kidnappings, rapes, murders and abuse of children and concerns for germs, diseases, and influence from the media, I'm thinking twice about it. I don't want to have children just to have to constantly worry about them in this world and worrying that somebody out there might harm them.

With all those things that I am learning from "real world" education, my advice is we all have a lot that I've got to keep in mind and one is to keep doors and windows locked at all times, never open the door for anyone unless you're expecting them.

Also be aware of your surroundings when you're at work or out in public because criminals are opportunist that target people. Keep your car door and windows locked, leave your room door open and be on the lookout when you are home by yourself.

Never give out personal information to just anyone from the street especially when it has to do with social security, credit card information or even your home address at that. Always be careful to not be in the wrong place at the wrong time.

With all that in mind, I heed those warnings and stay safe as a result. With that being said, there are some things that I like to be entertained by when I am either on my phone or on my computer. I like watching shows like Law and Order, National Geographic shows, Pippi Longs Stocking, Arthur, Elmo's World, Worst Nightmare on Discovery Channel, or things that catches my eye as long as it's not gory or demonic.

I do not like watching extreme scary scenes where people are possessed and acting demonic. I prefer watching shows that are fun, educational, and fascinating. With all the things that are shown on the screen such as beautiful scenery from different places, countries and states there is a lot to choose from.

For example, I checked out a video of an American Canyon mountain in Arizona and Colorado on National Geographic and it was a movie that I enjoyed watching.

It showed beautiful scenery of the mountains and deserts from Arizona as well as the Colorado rivers that streamed from Arizona to Colorado with a crew member that was on a expedition traveling by canoe on that kind of river.

They were canoeing away on that river while being very careful to not fall on the river and get swept away by the current of that river. It was so much fun watching it that I imagined myself being at American Canyon just sightseeing and touring the whole state and that whole mountain as well.

Then I didn't want the movie to end because I was enjoying it and plus I was getting really comfortable and a little bit sleepy on the couch so much that I didn't want to do anything to turn it off and walk away, because I was hoping for it to be longer so that I could just stay on the couch and nap away.

I remember seeing the American Canyon mountain but I couldn't see all of it on an airplane because it was limited and the airplane was moving along so I didn't get a chance to see the whole thing. But when I saw it on the movie by National Geographic, that was when I saw the whole view and scenery of American Canyon and it was very breathtaking and enthralling as well. Speaking of breathtaking and enthralling.

Author: Chelby Morgan

Autistically Speaking

I like to watch movies by Globe trekker where I get to see different countries like Germany, Italy, New York, Spain, the Rockies United States, the Northwestern United States, Scandinavian countries such as Denmark, Sweden, Finland, and Norway, Canada, Florida, Australia. Antarctica, Alaska, Mexico, Carribean Islands, New Zealand, China, Japan, and different other countries that I find myself wishing to go to.

The more I start watching those movies with different countries to look at, I feel that I am being a little bit more educated on countries as well as the food, language, climate and culture. Learning about different cultures from different countries is something that I believe is important to learn because if you ever decide to leave the states and go to those countries with some cultures added to it, then you will be better prepared to go there and go by the culture so as not to offend them.

One of the things that are some of the cultures in different countries is when someone prepares and serves you food whether it be in their home or at a restaurant, you never want to disrespect them by talking about the food that you don't like or simply throwing it away because they will get offended at you and say something to you about it.

It is possible to politely decline, pretend to eat it or accept it with gratitude so that you won't offend anybody or possibly get kicked out of the house.

This I imagine could be worse for some tourists if they don't have any money for a hotel room due to hotels that are really expensive in those countries. So that being said, don't ever be offensive to those that have their own cultures especially if you are entering into their country.

The country that they live in is theirs and you are coming on their turf so must respect their country and culture and keep your opinions about it to yourself before you find yourself on their bad side.

I also have learned that in some countries like Africa, Barbados, Jamaica, Asia, Belize and other different continents of the country, there are some things that are completely taboo such as disrespect to your elders, graffiti, vandalism, littering, drugs, promiscuity, prostitution, provocative dress and grooming, profanity, laziness, and not getting a good education.

Some of those countries don't even have welfare or any social programs to begin with. We're spoiled in this country because we have social programs for disabled people veterans and welfare, food stamps and cash aid for those who have children until they can get a job and suitable housing. Countries who don't have any social programs really have to work hard and not play around with any jobs because if they lose their jobs, that's it for them.

You are basically on your own in those countries unless you have family to take care of you and have a really good education. Without a good education, you are bound for abject poverty.

In third world countries there is no middle class, you are either poor or rich. That is it, period. I saw people on TV who live in Countries with no social programs. They also work twice as hard to make a living. It is also harder for them to provide for their families.

I think is commendable of them because they don't expect handouts nor are they lazy. They don't sit around on the couch all day long and watch TV.

During business hours you won't see them playing PS5 or Nintendo Switch. They are truly hard working all day in some useful way. While some of us in America are spoiled because we have social programs and get taken care of, I don't want to forget about my fellow humans across the globe who work hard.

I like to work and not always rely on handouts to get me by in life. I don't ever want to burden anyone with having to take care of me. I like to make my own money and someday start a business provided that I have all my ducks in row. Sometimes I like to watch the news on either my phone or computer because I happen to be curious about what is going on around the world and even in my area. Then other times I don't like to watch the news when there are some topics that I don't care about because they are either boring or not newsworthy.

I still like to learn and be entertained by things that are very fascinating and educational. As long as life goes on, I will never stop learning.

CHAPTER 10

My Determination

My Determination

Hi! I'm back and I am more determined to stay firm and strong because I want to serve as an inspiration to other people with developmental disabilities and be a living example for them to look up to.

They need to know that someone out there is going through the same things that they are going through as far as their disabilities are concerned. They at times may feel like they are alone and stuck in the world by themselves so to speak, with the feeling that no one understands them enough to be able to relate to them.

But when they hear my story, they will truly know that they are not alone and that they can look for somebody to really relate to them so that they see that there is somebody out there that is going through the same things that they are going through.

The more they do that, the more they will be inspired to make themselves stronger and stay determined to be firm and fight to keep their heads up and not let anyone or anything stop them in the process.

If you have a developmental disability or a are parent/friend to an individual that has a mental disability, then please take comfort in what I am writing because this can truly benefit you. Okay we'll start off this way.

Autistically Speaking

I have autism and I am not ashamed to say it because for one thing, people need to know that I am not a dummy or a "retard" as I have been called. Im also not a dum dum that doesn't know anything or understand what is going on around me.

Being autistic does not mean that you are retarded because there proves to be a different connotation to those words and disabilities. The difference is because the word "retarded" means that depending on what type of retardation that you may have is that the person who has it may be a little bit slower in processing things and has a hard time retaining information that they read in books, magazines and textbooks.

Oh, case in point, I say normal people are retarded whenever they call other people with mental disabilities retarded. These type of people do whatever they can to bully and make us feel like they we are less than a person that they are.

I say they are retarded in a sense where they have no sensitivity or compassion for those that have brains that process information and thinking abilities a little bit different than what they think that their brains should process. They are all about going by the so-called normal standards that they themselves impose. They will make fun of the way we talk or dress. To them, we don't look pretty or attractive but to me, the bully is not pretty or attractive at all by the way they act and talk to others who are different.

Oh and even if they manage to look pretty or attractive on the outside, it is only according to standards they impose on themselves or other people. They must learn to be pretty on the inside because pretty soon all the pretty looks that they keep for themselves will fade away as they get older and they will be left with nothing to look forward to. So in a nutshell, don't be ugly to anybody or you will find yourself with ugly truth that you have no friends at all because you are ugly.

Everyone knows God don't like ugly and he made us all equal. So that being the case, he treats everyone with respect and dignity and says all humans deserve to be treated nice. So in return he expects us to do the same but if he sees us being ugly to other people who have any kind of disabilities on them, then he is not very happy about that and doesn't treat anybody like that himself. Furthermore when he sees that we're being ugly to other people by calling them "stupid" and "retarded", making fun of the way they talk, dress and look, excluding them from groups and even beating them up, then he will turn his face away from them and help you instead.

It doesn't please me to see people be ugly to those who have disabilities. When I was in school I used to be on the receiving end of some kids' ugly attitudes, speech and comments about me being handicapped, fat and retarded. It was so bad that it would make me very mad and it would make me want to fight back because I didn't think that was nice at all.

Author: Chelby Morgan

Even tho I am different, they still don't have that right to demean, degrade and belittle in any kind of way. I think everyone should treat each other the way they themselves would like to be treated. In the future they might need them on cars, plumbing, entertainment, or to save their behinds from a fire.

So never treat anyone like they're less than nothing. What if when the person you bully gets older, they become successful in what they do? They can become a CEO or even managing their own businesses while you might find yourself on the receiving end of being desperate in search of a suitable job. What if when you go to a businesses to get hired, you find yourself working for the same people that you got done labeling as "ugly", "retarded" and "stupid" in school? This is why no one should be ugly or call names and make fun of them to begin with.

So if you are or were the person who acted ugly, you might want to start treating everyone with more respect and dignity. Second of all, I may think and process things differently than what most so-called normal people do, but have a laden amount of patience, compassion and long-suffering for everyone with a disability will help you to understand we have the same likes, dislikes, traits, personalities, hobbies, places to go, favorite colors, and even goals that everyone else in the world wants to accomplish in life.

I say never be quick to write anyone off as if they are not intelligent or capable of thinking or understanding what is going on around them. Besides one never knows when will need anyone in a time of crisis.

What if your car breaks down and you find yourself being held captive by a kidnapper who is bent on holding you hostage until he or she is ready to get rid of you. You then see the person you called retarded walk by. You then say help me. Call the police but the kidnapper says something polite like, hello mam, how are you doing. Don't mind me please have a nice day.

Would you want me to call 911 for you or will I remember that you treated me like a door mat when you find yourself in a jam? I probably would remember the way you treated me in high school and my impulse would be to decide not to help you at all because of all the bad things you said about me. What goes around comes right back around.

With me even though I feel that way, I will be willing enough to help you and I would tell the kidnapper that I am a citizen and will call 911 and demand that he release you. But I also will tell you that once the kidnapper lets you go if you take advantage of me again, I might not stop to help you out the next time.

Despite my autism I am not dumb because I am able to care for myself and help my family. I help around the house with different chores. I do yard work and vacuuming out the car to keep it clean. When things are clean, it makes me feel good for doing it in the first place and makes me comfortable.

Speaking of comfortable, the van that we have in the garage is so cozy, homely and comfy because it fits everyone comfortably and we can move around in it freely with plenty of leg room. We had vans for many years and it served us very well in getting us around.

I like being inside vehicles because I get to listen to my favorite songs on CDs and on my mom's cell-phone and one of my favorite songs that she likes to play is one about San Jose and about this one singer who talks about what she wants her man to cook for her and keep himself waiting on her hand and foot as well as to amuse her or lose her. I like that part because it is so cute and funny at the same time

I don't know if I want to try that in any relationships that I encounter because to be the one in control especially in relationships is not my favorite thing to do. I don't think any relationships should be about control and waiting on one partner hand and foot and just doing what one partner wants them to do. It just wouldn't work and after a while it gets to a point where it gets old and not cute anymore.

With me I don't think it's cute at all because I feel that relationships should exist on love and not on control and slavery. Oh and speaking of relationships, I am very open to starting relationships but I am not quick to get into one right now because I am waiting for the right man to come along and sweep me off of my feet for real and not fake it.

This one man came along and thought he was all that. He said all the ladies said he was a pretty boy in high school. I told him somebody done told him wrong and that he needs to look a little hotter for me.

For now I am going to keep on waiting until the right time to start a relationship because right now is not a good time especially with the corona virus. I thought Cornona was beer. Anyway I have friends and family that helps keep me on the right track in life and they do not put pressure on me to date or get married.

When dating or considering marriage, it doesn't matter how much money, good looks, possessions, or status that a guy may have, if he doesn't have desirable traits such as having respect for women and not beating on them or expecting them to be a certain weight, his slave, then he can forget about it and can be miserable by himself.

I am not about to settle for any man that is all about himself or thinks cheating or beating on women is ok.

Those are the same ones that wouldn't pick on someone their own size and know the consequence for doing so which is getting beat doubly.

I think that's why they take their frustration and anger on women that they date or marry.

How will I know if a man is suitable enough for me? Can I discern the red flags? I do process of elimination. For example, this is a red flag. If a man is single and talks about the women he divorced or break up with, then that is a red flag for me.

Or if there are two or more different women who have previously dated the same guy that now wants to date or marry me, and the other two said he cheated on them, or verbally assaulted them or beaten them up, then that is a red flag and he will have to kiss the possibility of a relationship with me goodbye.

That is not acceptable to me at all. I expect better than that because I am not somebody that can be walked all over and treated like that.

I might sometimes sound dumb, but im not dumb like some guys may think I am. When they do that, it is to try to intimidate me or to get me to compromise on things I said I don't compromise on. It won't happen because I will be staying far away from them.

Plus I am not the one for them and will type this only once as a lesson and that is, DO NOT ASK ME TO GO ON a dates or marry you.

I am not ready to do so and I clearly do not want to be with someone that I am not interested in.

I don't want to disappoint you but it will only get you disappointment to ask and get a polite rejection.

I don't depend on guys for happiness or attention even though they can be dominant. There are other things to make me happy and attract my attention. If I go on a date it is not all about me wearing a certain clothing style that reveals my body. I will wear modest attire. It will be cute but not be so short that it shows off my beautiful legs and stomach.

Some guys insist that girls wear high heels for a date. That is shallow and not funny because a date isn't about wearing heels. Men don't realize wearing high heels can make our feet hurt. It would ache throughout the whole date and w'd be miserable throughout it all. If I was on a date and had to wear heels I then would ask him to carry me since he insisted on me wearing high heels in the first. That'll probably teach him a lesson in not insisting that I wear heels in the first place, because I weigh 155 pounds give or take and if he can't lift me I will talk about him.

So the moral of that lesson is never insist that your date wears heels on the whole date and you won't have to be forced to carry her in the first place in an event where her feet starting hurting throughout the whole event.

In a nutshell, I am waiting until the Mr. Right comes along my way and that may take a while but it is worth the wait and doesn't bother me. I have so much else to focus on in the meantime. I like to travel and I got a chance to do that. I went to L.A. and had the best time of my life by going to Universal Studios and Magic Mountain as well as Disney land which I didn't care for as much. But I had the best time of my life.

Then I got to travel to New York and see Manhattan, Times Square, China Town, Patterson and Brooklyn. Manhattan was the best with central park and a nice hamburger restaurant to top it off. Manhattan had the best central park that people would kill to go to at any time for it is a nice haven for joggers, homeless people, and other people that just want to relax and get away from it all. It is also home to a zoo and was really hot and stuffy over there.

If anyone ever gets across to going to Manhattan please either avoid the zoo or go at your own risk. New York is always fast and busy and never sleeps, so if you need to get some things taken care of before midnight please do so.

New York is not for everyone and If you can't hang out all night don't go there. But for those who like to explore and go on adventures, then try New York for what I call a "square root 1" adventure as a way to take it one step at a time.

If you decide you want to take the biggest step to different countries like say Spain, Turkey, South Africa and maybe Moroccan which I thought about going because of a little bit of the spices and middle eastern music and culture they have to offer, Morrocan is on my list.

I thought I didn't want to go to Morocco at first but now it turns out that I would love to try out Morocco. If need be, I would sleep on top of a Moroccan roof to save money on hotel and look at the natural beauty of the stars that twinkled in the sky.

Then after a night or few nights of sleeping on top of the roof, I would get down from the roof and do some sightseeing and meet some amazing locals on the way. Even though tourists can wear cloths without burkas or veils, I still want to be mindful with the way I dress because I definitely do not want to draw unnecessary attention to myself by the way I dressed.

When I travel, this is my thing I like to wear. I weak flats or tennis shoes instead of wearing heels because I will be doing a lot of walking, so I don't want my feet to be hurting or have fatigue at that.

I find that my trip proves to be a lot more fun when my shoes are very comfortable to wear and walk in. When I went to New York, we did a lot of walking, so I wore a lot of flats and gym shoes and in that way, I felt very comfortable and my trip proved to be very fun and enjoyable.

I didn't even complain about my feet hurting in the first place. My thing is people that walk in heels in New York, especially in metropolitan areas because they want to look cute were not happy campers.

That wasn't the case for me because I did not want sores or aching feet to begin with not to mention I looked cute and hot without heels. If you do a lot of walking in places like New York, having on high heels wont work, trust me. You also have to be careful if you wear heels.

If you must wear heels, make sure they are the ones meant for comfort because the last thing you want to do is go barefoot on a dirty floor in a metropolitan area. The floors and streets are always dirty and carry a lot of dirty germs.

Oh speaking of dirty city floors, an area called China Town in New York is notorious for rats, so if you go there, be very cautious for rats because they are very gross and disgusting and that is not the type of ground that you want to even walk barefoot on in the first place.

Being barefoot is not an option for me in the first place. I have seen people cut their feet on glass while walking in different areas of their neighborhood while being barefoot.

Some people go barefoot and I don't know how they do it on a nasty ground but if it were me, I would be appalled to do it because I do not want to stick my feet on dirty ground and find myself with ringworm down the road of my lifetime. Ringworm is fungi and filled with germs.

If you get it no one will want to be around you. When I go out or happen to check the mail, I will put on sandals. I feel I have something on my feet at least. Even though im only going from my house to the mailbox the ground is still the ground and I am not trying to get any germs on my feet or get ringworm.

I'm religious about checking the mail because I like to check it and see if something has come in the mail for me such as a letter from a friend or important documents. I also look for written notices or stuff that I might need to sign. I might even have orders coming in the mail for me. I like mail because seeing my name on mail is like getting a special gift in the mail just for me.

Sometimes I will order things on Amazon to save myself the trip of going to a store to buy stuff that I need. I feel that if it can get delivered to my home and I receive the product by mail, then why not. I also order online because it saves my Dad or mom having to drive me to get it.

Speaking of driving, my uncle let me drive his Mercedes Benz. He treated me normal and let me drive around the city I live in.

It was so fun. His car talked and seemed to do everything for me. He was on the phone laughing and having a good ol time and I was to. I told him that I am moving up in life and may one day be married. We chit chatted.

I often wondered why he let me drive his car that I later found out from google cost allot of money. When I asked him why did he let me drive his expensive car, he said that he wants me to drive the best he has to offer me. He also said, he wanted to demonstrate how a man by his action will make it clear if they are giving me their very best.

He then went back to our conversation we had in while I was driving, about selecting a marriage mate and how I should look for a person that always gives their very best in all areas of life and such a person would be as evident as it was to me when I was driving around town in my dream car.

Lately since the pandemic I thought of driving more but I been putting it off because I feel I am not ready now during this pandemic. Plus a lot of crazy people drive like maniacs and cause accidents which is why I see people always honking and being impatient and wanting to always be the first to go at a green light.

Sometimes when I am in the car with my mom, it frustrates her when other people drives fast just to get to a green light and not stop at a "Yield" sign. People forget that other cars need to get by smoothly without the worry of being in a car accident.

There are some that know that you are coming but still dart out into the street just to get by where they supposedly need to go instead of being patient enough to wait their turn.

That really annoys me because if they cause an accident and injure somebody in the process, then they probably would run away from it all and act like it never happened. I am thinking about driving but will only do it after the pandemic and if I need to go on a road trip with some friends to different states like Idaho, Tennessee, Louisiana, and other exciting states that have come up on my mind a few times.

Place that I would like to see on my list is Idaho because that's where the potatoes are and I just happen to want to get me some potatoes right now. Then I would like to see some locals and visit a potato farm at that.

It may be in the middle of nowhere but hey there are some things that I would like to see for their beautiful scenery, nice houses. I think about taking a hike on some mountains in Idaho as well. Besides I hear it is somewhere quiet, slow and laidback there instead of always being about party scenes and clubbing with loud music and noise.

Next on my list is Washington because of some beautiful grass that the state possess resulting from the rain. Picky me will not go when it is raining because I hate rain and anything that causes me to be soaking wet in imminent weather.

Author: Chelby Morgan

Then I want to check out this French restaurant because they offer some nice food and French bakery at that.

After I get done eating, then I want to visit some museums that educate me on Indian history and visit some of their teepees as well before going off to a concern with nice jazzy music and saxophones to top it off. Next state to visit is Alabama because when I visited that place, I saw only a little bit, so if I get a chance to go there, I want to see a whole lot of places such as Birmingham, Huntsville, Montgomery and Monroeville and see some of the houses that look like the houses that I saw on How to Kill A Mockingbird. Those houses are very classic and memorable to think about when you get to be in a moment of thought like I do.

Those houses that look like the houses on How to Kill A Mockingbird are the same ones that are either for rent or sale. I don't think that I would live there unless I could inherit my grandmother's country house where she has hundreds of acres and a forest of trees that the people offer to buy from her land but she said no.

There are other different states that I would love to drive to. I guess after the pandemic I will start learning more on driving so I can take a road trip and go on different adventures.

As I get older, I get used to having a disability because I am going to have to deal with it for life so I make the best out of my situation or anything that has to do with autism.

I used to think about what it would be like to have autism when I got older, but now that I am here, I don't see it as a disability because I have truly learned to get around it and think positive.

I have my own sayings now and call it **PLL** it stands for Personal Life List. I think my Personal Life List is necessary to have as I use it to get around my disability and live life to the full. My PLL has a list of twelve things to make anyone successful.

PLL

(1) Pray to the most High God.

(2) Keep family first because they always love you.

(3) Always love yourself and others.

(4) Stay positive and write things down. It relieves negative feelings.

(5) Keep tight reigns on your social life.

(6) Keep a lookout for human sharks.

(7) Magnify abilities you have to make up for ones you don't have.

(8) Ignore people who are negative but show pity for them.

(9) Work out and read good books. Healthy mind, healthy body.

(10) Master hobbies because it could become your career.

(11) Always keep a sense of humor.

(12) Care for your parents as they age.

If you keep my PLL list of 12 items in mind, it will help you succeed in life. How do I know, because it helps me every day and gives me the hope to know I have potential to do anything.

Autistically Speaking

I believe I can do anything I put my mind to. I had an aide appointed to me by the state of California who was more than just an aide, she was like a step mother who has the same confidence in me as my mom and dad and family.

My aide didn't view me as stupid or a lost cause because I do not think or processing things they way some others think I should process some information. I was somebody she saw as being smart with real talent, good thinking faculties and the capability to think for myself and not let others take advantage of me.

One time when I told her that I didn't like math, she told me that if I had to do math for a job I would need it to learn how to do math and count cash to do the job effectively. If I didn't learn math customer could jip me into giving the wrong amount of cash back for an order or a product.

My uncle on the other hand told me that I just better start liking math and I would be happy about it later. He always had a way of saying things how they are and I like that about him.

I never did like math but I sure am glad that I learned it as it does help me in life.

I don't have to do it for a grade but I used it at when I was a cashier at McDonalds fast food restaurant. I really started to appreciate the math I learned in high school and enjoyed it.

When I had to learn the cash register I already knew how to count change, and it was not that big of a shock for me. I valued the patience that my teacher, aide and family had for me when I was on my job at the fast food restaurant. One thing about a fast food restaurant is you have to learn the cash register fast because it's fast food and you must be fast in giving back change.

The people who ran the fast food restaurant expected you to get the hang of everything fast and that did prove to be frustrating for me because apparently what I think is fast is really slow in the real world. It only became complicated when they said I was not fast enough.

So I eventually decided to quit McDonalds because I just felt like it wasn't for me. There was some lessons that did learn when I walked out of the fast food restaurant job. I learned how to be more patient with certain people who want to be nothing but jerks. I learned how to make peace with others and not always having something to say back to people.

It doesn't always go well if you say things back. I learned a good lesson in working with the public and learning how to deal effectively with other people especially if they are very rude and demanding. I learned that customers are always going to be customers so you must learn to keep your cool under pressure and remain composed even when you are provoked.

Author: Chelby Morgan

I really needed some composure in the area of compose because some people provoked me and were rude in a few different ways to the point where I wanted to throw ice cream on them to make them snap out of it. Throughout my life I come to realize people may always provoke you or get on your nerves. You will need to learn how to effectively deal with it.

On the other hand if I didn't learn to deal with rude people and not respond in kind to those that were provoking me or getting on my nerves, I would probably have gone off on them or end up getting in an altercation. I am so thankful that I did not return insult or respond to those who provoked or taunted me. I just don't feel it's necessary to do that to get your point across to somebody. Sometimes ignoring a person or simply talking to them about the situation proves to be a little more effective than the opposite that I mentioned.

I now feel confident in the area of social skills. Some of my abilities allow me to take care of my business and plan a schedule for each day that I wake up in the morning. I am thankful to wake up alive and get out of bed with no other problems or complications and believe it is truly a blessing to enjoy the life you have. I like to accomplish things that are needing attention.

After I accomplish things that need my attention it makes me feel good about it because the things that I accomplish are less things that I have to accomplish in the near future and I am happy for that. I really love my life that I have and would never change for that for the world.

There are many people that I want to give credit to for my successful life. I will never forget my former aide. She was one who pushed me to do my best and also saw the good potential in me. She said she thought I couldn't accomplish more than I even knew I could.

Although we didn't always see eye to eye on everything, we were always on good terms and had each other as best friends to talk to and walk to classes together. She was easygoing and laid back with a good sense of humor.

She was not the kind to always to be serious about school and school related items only. When there was time to laugh, joke and play around a bit, she did so and I always felt at ease. I enjoyed the times that we had together and when I had to move away from her, it was really hard to adjust because I really enjoyed her and considered her like family.

I even wished she went with me to high school so it could have been easier for me to deal with the constant pressures and issues that came with high school.

Author: Chelby Morgan

I hated the feeling of always trying to fit in with people that I thought were my friends and then later found out they were not. She would've been on my side and genuinely would have looked out and protect me from those who were out to mess with me or beat me up.

In fact she knew how to protect me and put some heat into their behinds if they ever came near to mess with or harm me in any way. Even bullies would know to stay away from me because they wouldn't want to hear her mouth or experience the consequences.

Even when I was away from her, I would have the protection of going to her because I knew that I could count on her to do the mama bear job for me and she would not play around with it either. She would make sure that they got the point real fast enough to save themselves from any further disciplinary action from either her or the school staff because the school staff that I had in Georgia was very strict against bullying.

For those who don't know an aide goes to school with some autistic people in order to prevent us from getting taken advantage. It's like the President who has secret service with them all the time. I always had an aide with me in school. Without an aide for autistic people, it would have been even worse.

Although I don't have that kind of protection anymore, the best protection that I now have is what I learned over the years and the fortress of my family and friends who help me to on decision and when to ignore people who are rude or out to provoke me or ways to effectively settle disputes without having to use violence or profanity.

Sometimes I want to go back and change some of the things from my past but I can't so I learn to make the best of my situation and focus on moving forward into the future.

In fact, I am focused on moving forward with my book writing career as well as some future goals to set up a website for disabled adults and start a few businesses as well. I think I can do it and therefore I am determined to follow through with my goals and pursue them as well. I am truly determined to keep my head up, look towards the future and be determined to stay firm and strong despite having a disability.

I have learned allot about myself and one of them is being happy and content with myself. It is not possible to be somebody else because you are you. If you try to be someone else then you will only fail at being someone else miserably.

Autism has taught me to love myself a little bit better and really be thankful that I can still function as a normal as an adult and human as I can.

Author: Chelby Morgan

Autistically Speaking

There are people with developmental disabilities that just can't do much by themselves and are basically trapped in their own bodies. Sometimes I visualize what it would be like to not have autism but reality says that it is still there so I make the best of my situation and stay positive.

I also stay upbeat. I physically, emotionally, and mentally keep myself active and do not sit around and feel sorry and depressed about myself. Even if I could feel sorry for myself it would not accomplish anything because I would still have my condition.

I am also inspired by other people who have different disabilities such as blindness, deafness, physical disabilities, cancer, Down Syndrome and other mental disabilities.

Sadly some people with those disabilities may feel they are not smart or could live successful lives, but they would be wrong, look at Helen Keller. She was blind and deaf with everyone around her thinking that she was soft-brained and dumb without being able to communicate, but she was able to prove them all wrong by earning a degree and becoming a famous author.

Now tell me if that is the sign of a dumb or soft-brained person? I don't think so. Blind or deaf people are not dumb nor do they want to be viewed as such. If they can think for themselves and strive to live happy and successful lives with determination, trust and believe they will accomplish anything with all their strength and might. Whatever it takes.

Helen Keller helps in keeping me going without giving up or feeling sorry for myself. In case I do want to feel sorry for myself and just give up, I am reminded of the goals that I want to pursue and how other people with more severe disabilities are doing more than I am with zeal and determination. So my kind of disability is nothing in comparison.

If they can do more things despite their limitations with determination, then who am I to say that I won't do something with determination and keep myself going. Autism is just a name for me because I don't see myself as the girl with autism. I see myself as a woman who is overcoming her challenges and doing so gracefully.

A woman who is very strong and can handle herself quite well. So that's another thing that I learned about myself and will continue to learn as this life goes on. I also learned the value of controlling my emotions. If I were to give into my emotions, then I would be learning life's lessons the hard way. During my youth I used to show feelings such as jealousy for once and shudder to think what would happen if I gave into that feeling and acted on it. So therefore I am really glad that I don't have jealousy for anybody.

I am happy with who I am on both the outside and inside. I don't feel that it's necessary for me to look like or be somebody else for we all look and think differently than most people. Also as an adult I am very thankful for all the tools that people who I love in my life have given me the survive in the real world.

Author: Chelby Morgan

My biggest people I want to credit is my parents because if they didn't help me to push myself a little bit more, I would not have been able to reach all of my potential. I am more than thankful for what they have done for me.

The older I get the more I see a light at the end of every tunnel that I go through. Being an adult truly works out well for me. For example, I've learned that jealousy is rotten to the bones and when I think about that more often, I think of a character named Cain who gave into feelings of jealousy and anger to the point where he killed his brother Abel in the fields.

What was so sad about that was he did not show any remorse until he was caught and at risk of someone else taking vengeance on him because of what he did to Abel.

I see allot of people at work jealous of the boss of what someone has or does not have. I never want to be jealous of anybody. If I allow myself to become jealous of somebody because of their looks, status, finances, or they wore, it would consume me and cause me to have rotten trait called ugliness.

I also don't want to have animosity toward anyone to any point of wanting to do away with them. I strive to make peace with everyone in life. I speak politely and respectfully to everyone.

Me staying busy with projects like studying, book writing, typing on Mavis, learning a new language, traveling, and spending time with family and friends keeps me from becoming jealous. Jealous is also counterproductive and you will loose sleep and health over it for that matter.

Another thing that I have learned about myself is that I do not need the "bad boy" persona in my life as a mate. I feel I can do way better than marrying the bad boy persona who would not have my best interest at heart nor remain loyal and faithful to me.

At work I have seen this one boy which is what I will call him, because he didn't act like a man, get all up in this one girls face and tell her what she wanted to hear and how he wants to be her boyfriend for life. But literally a month after they hooked up, she told me she has a kid on the way and hates him.

She said he treated her like a hood rat and that he has two baby mommas and that she only knew about one of them. She told me always be careful and not to make the same mistake she made because she is paying for it every day now.

If it were me and I knew he had one baby mama, I wouldn't have considered him because I don't have time for the drama or the baby momma.

My thing is a guy who is a thug or deadbeat dad is not something that I am impressed with because they are just a bunch of knuckleheads and bums who are just too lazy to do anything for the girl and the kids that they claim they love.

Some girls like guys that are thuggish due to low self-esteem or not feeling loved or accepted by family or friends. I'm glad that such is not the case with me. If I don't find the absolute best or the absolute best does not find me, I prefer to be single and am happy with the way it is.

Besides all that, I am too busy advocating for people with autism through my book. We all are humans with a right to be treated with respect and dignity like every other human being should be treated.

I want to also give credit to my grandmother who always said to me and I wrote it down "everyone has potential, but until it is paired with a Purpose it lays dormant." She also said I should put my potential to work by having a purpose in life and I will be able to accomplish anything.

She would know because she is a University Professor of Psychology and a famous book published author. She is one of my inspirations. She has books all over the world and is in the library of congress. She is very special to me and I love her very much. I love you nanny.

Autistically Speaking

Well remember how I told you that I love movies with good endings. My life story has shifted gears. I must be special because as you are reading my book, it has gone viral. I am not a published author. I cant believe this.

My books are in over 190 Countries around the world and I am in 40,000 stores around the world.

My Publishers are even talking to people about my life and want to consider my story on a Lifetime original.

I want everyone to know. If I sell one book or a million books, I will still be your friend and you are still my friend.

If I didn't name you in my book don't worry, I have other books coming out and will include you in those. My Publisher contracted me to do three books, and I have a website so feel free to reach out to me if you want to.

Also don't be afraid to use spell check or in Microsoft word. It really has helped me in my book.

Visit my website to contact me at **www.chelbymorgan.com** if you want to see what next on my life list. Even if you are the girls and boys who bullied me, you still can write me and I forgive you.

I really cant believe that I get paid to write about my life like this. I am not going to quit my job though and be all high society. I love working and all of the free stuff I get now. I will thank all of these companies who send me free stuff for my opinion. I will talk about you all in my next book.

Author: Chelby Morgan

How To Be Successful

How To Be Successful

To be successful, all it takes is a little effort.

To all parents of my fellow peers who may also live with the diagnosis of autism, I hope after you read this book you will see the most important factor to your child's success is love. Love is what inspires us to exceed our ~~dis~~**Ability**.

~ *THE END* ~

Author: Chelby Morgan

CPSIA information can be obtained
at www.ICGtesting.com
Printed in the USA
LVHW040058121220
673919LV00006B/278

9 781619 100305